# ¡Verdura!

## Living a Garden Life

# ¡Verdura!
## Living a Garden Life

## 30 PROJECTS
to Nurture Your Passion for Plants & Find Your Bliss

PERLA SOFÍA CURBELO-SANTIAGO

COOL
SPRINGS
PRESS

**Quarto.com**

© 2023 Quarto Publishing Group USA Inc.
Text © 2023 Zurda Media Enterprises, Inc.
Photography © 2023 Quarto Publishing
Group USA Inc.

First Published in 2023 by Cool Springs Press,
an imprint of The Quarto Group,
100 Cummings Center, Suite 265-D,
Beverly, MA 01915, USA.
T (978) 282-9590  F (978) 283-2742

Cool Springs Press titles are also available at dis-
count for retail, wholesale, promotional, and bulk
purchase. For details, contact the Special Sales
Manager by email at specialsales@quarto.com or
by mail at The Quarto Group, Attn: Special Sales
Manager, 100 Cummings Center, Suite 265-D,
Beverly, MA 01915, USA.

27 26 25 24 23    1 2 3 4 5

ISBN: 978-0-7603-8126-7

Digital edition published in 2023
eISBN: 978-0-7603-8127-4

The Spanish version of this book, *¡Verdura! –
Jardinería para tu bienestar*, was published in
2023 under ISBN 978-0-7603-8271-4 (paperback)
and 978-0-7603-8272-1 (ebook).

Library of Congress Cataloging-in-Publication
Data available.

Design and page layout: Laura Shaw Design
Cover Images: Jorge Ramirez Portela
Photography: Jorge Ramirez Portela , except
those by Perla Sofía Curbelo-Santiago (pages 5,
10, 48 [top two], 68, 77, 113 [top], 117) and Luis
Ángel Curbelo Rodríguez (page 15).
Illustration: Julia Dreams and Shutterstock
(parchment paper background)

Printed in China

To my parents, Hilda and Luis Ángel, for giving me love, wings, ground, books, art, and a backyard to play in with my two brothers.

And to my beloved Antonio and my dear Sofía and Verónica, for cultivating a joyful life together.

Perla Sofía, age 3

# Contents

# Gardening Projects

# Preface

THE BEST GARDEN always will be the one you have. Even if is just one well-tended houseplant or a tiny vegetable garden on a windowsill that produces enough ingredients to make your favorite bruschetta.

For a long time, I thought my garden space wasn't green or colorful enough to show off, except for an occasional post on my website or social media. Certainly, never for a book. And yet here we are. You're holding my first book, which features thirty gardening projects—*verduras*—photographed in and around my home and garden in Puerto Rico. I can assure you that a lot of sweat, laughter, and tears went into it, but the result is immensely satisfying.

To get here, I had to overcome the well-known adage of "the grass is always greener on the other side." From the beginning, right after I said yes to this editorial endeavor, I thought of many places in Puerto Rico, including friends' and family's homes that were suitable for shooting the images in this book, never thinking of my garden as an option.

After my Plan A to use a friend's garden space to photograph the first few projects fell through, (and, honestly, I didn't have a well-thought-out Plan B to fall back on) my garden came to the rescue, as it always has. I was already using it for my personal well-being, and some of my personal and professional gardening projects were featured, close-framed, on social media, but nothing like utilizing or transforming bigger areas to use as a backdrop for other small projects, or to be the big project itself. I can tell you now that the amount of effort put into my garden for a total of eight months was all worth it.

As you go through these pages, you will notice some of the gardening project ideas, particularly those on the patio, are in close proximity to each other. Some of the indoor projects, too. Right after the first photo shoot, which went well for a not-so-backup plan, I realized that because there were going to be so many projects in the book, I needed to come up with a better plan to present them all while still making them relatable for the reader to replicate, and easy for me to coordinate on a budget. So, I used this amazing opportunity to give my garden, and various indoor spaces, a makeover.

Yes, this is a personal editorial project—from the stories I share as an introduction to most of the gardening, crafts, and how-to ideas, to the space where I live with my husband and dog. Not only were the projects to be interesting, exciting, and, alluring for the reader but also practical to me to keep around for further enjoyment.

This incredible garden-based adventure validated so many things for me—from the power of nature and the act of gardening as a wellness path to the importance of assigning a purpose to your gardening activities.

There are many things in our daily lives that we want or need to get done, including past-due gardening projects, but sometimes we are hesitant or unsure how to tackle them with limited resources.

Know this, when you give a project a purpose and make it personal (this can be applied to anything), you follow through no matter how tough or distant the finish line may seem. You become even more creative.

Of course, I still love a picture-perfect garden, but even those have to start somewhere, one container at a time. Now, I must tell you, there is no other garden I would rather be in and have than mine. Visit your local garden center, explore secondhand stores, your neighborhood, and all your closets looking for plants, objects, and accessories that will make your project resonate with who you are right where you are.

It's not about perfection, otherwise I would not be here having this conversation with you, but rather paying attention to what you already have, meaning yours is already the best.

# Introduction

The Most Important Part of a Garden Is the One Who Enjoys It

*Gift of the Amherst Garden Club*

Unknown author

A FEW YEARS AGO while on a garden tour at the Buffalo and Erie County Botanical Gardens in New York, I spotted a little sign in front of a potted begonia that read, "The most important part of a garden is the one who enjoys it." I snapped a photo and continued with the tour through the begonia collection. It was August 2017.

I forgot about the picture until a couple years later when I was preparing for a conference in Puerto Rico about the benefits of gardening, and came across it—everything suddenly started to make sense.

From early in my life, I was drawn to playing outdoors and being in contact with nature. From walking shoeless in my parents' backyard to climbing, almost daily, the front yard pink trumpet tree (*Tabebuia rosea*). Later, as I grew older, probably between ten and twelve, I would go around the neighborhood peeking into people's gardens to see what kind of beautiful plants and flowers were growing there. Most of the time I would ask for specific flowers, such as roses. I brought the plants collected back home to make little bouquets and placed them in my room or on the family dinner table.

Being in the presence of flowers, plants, or trees always felt magical and natural to me. So, it doesn't surprise me at all to have chosen, after a few bumps along my professional road, today's path as a garden communicator. I can spend long hours thinking, reading, and talking about the joys and other benefits that plants brings into our lives.

Nowadays, this is why I garden: to create a moment in time that I can enjoy first, because, somehow, the rest will follow—the flowers, the produce, the health benefits, and the satisfying daily habit.

My experience as a garden communicator has given me the amazing opportunity to talk to many plant professionals and, most important, to other plant lovers.

For some, their experiences with plants were first through someone else's green thumb, such as parents or grandparents. Acts, supposedly, difficult to follow. Some tales, heard repeatedly, were about feelings of frustration because everything died in their hands, even cacti. Gardening projects were just another source of stress in their lives. Of course, I could relate to that. As I, too, imposed high gardening standards on myself that predicted an abundant yield of frustration with no joy at all. That is when I came to the realization that we were not necessarily putting ourselves into the gardening equation.

Generally, when we garden, everything is focused on the plant's needs: light, water, fertilizer. But, what about our needs?

When most of us bring a new plant into our lives, including creating a veggie garden, we tend to skip an important consideration: understanding our lifestyle. For some, the urge to *green up* the space gives us more stress instead of more joy.

Learning about who we are, our tastes, and what makes us comfortable, is as important as getting to know each plant's requirements. This is putting ourselves in a favorable position when gardening. Of course, there will be frustrations in between the successes, but the recovery from these and return to our starting sanity point will be faster. For me, planning my gardening experiences has been a key.

If we take time to plan our gardening experiences (yes, leave others to spontaneity) we might end up increasing the enjoyment potential of the project and, hopefully, want to repeat and explore further gardening and nature-based activities.

*Verdura* was inspired by an annual digital series on *Agrochic,* a website I founded in 2009. "Verdura" means "greenery" in Spanish, but also refers to any edible plant sown in the garden, like lettuce, kale, or radish leaves. In Puerto Rico, we prefer to apply *verduras* to boiled root plants such as yuca, malanga, ñame, or batata, and green bananas, too, served alone or as a side dish.

For this book, I use *verdura* as a description and aspiration: adding more *verdura* to our daily life. Most plants are green, and it is well-known that this color is associated with calmness and tranquility, as well as prosperity, a good life, and being outdoorsy.

The thirty projects here are for you to experience your way. I share the basic components to inspire you to get out there and plan your gardening activity, taking into consideration your resources; including where you are emotionally, physically, and geographically. Because, as in a garden, the most important part of *this* book is for you to enjoy it.

—PERLA SOFÍA

# Explore Nature

Years before I stepped foot for the first time on a plane (I was twenty-one) to start exploring new countries, I already knew about the most fascinating places in the world.

BOOKS, ART, MOVIES, television, and people took me there.

As kids, my brothers and I played and explored the limits of our parents' backyard patio. As we grew, we were allowed to hang out with other kids on our street, and, later on, the whole neighborhood. I loved to peek into people's yards to see which plants were growing and, maybe, taking one or two back home (with permission, of course).

First, I went around on foot scanning people's front yard patios looking for any kind of roses. Later, I used my bike to explore. Having a bicycle meant the freedom to explore places other than my own. Sometimes, I dared to bike to distant locations, half an hour from home, with friends, and by myself, too. Just the act of cycling felt adventurous.

I grew up in the 1980s. Movies such as *E.T. the Extra-Terrestrial*, *The Goonies*, and *Indiana Jones* were some of the box office hits of the decade. They modeled, for me and my generation, how cool it was to explore and learn about new cultures and get acquainted and be able to communicate with strange characters, from this world or out of it. There was no dentist's office we visited that didn't have the iconic *National Geographic* magazine pile. I still bow to its pages, filled with spectacular photography and interesting articles about recent discoveries of plants, or what was causing harm to certain species.

It was during that period, too, that I began to be interested in learning other languages and collecting stamps and coins. I even joined a pen pal program with kids of my age and enjoyed watching the renowned French explorer and a pioneer of the marine conservancy, Jacques Cousteau, on TV.

Research tells us that exploring nature, in any way, contributes to the development of our brains as well as to our physical and emotional health. For kids, nature provides numerous opportunities to discover new and exciting experiences that encourage them to learn by doing.

As adults, exploring nature can help us feel more relaxed and facilitate creative problem solving. Nowadays, health organizations encourage older adults to participate more often in any kind of nature-exploring experiences to promote cognitive enhancement, body movement, and social connection. When we're less stressed, we rest better, which strengthens our immune system and increases our resistance to disease.

This group of gardening projects is meant for you to have fun exploring nature around you, in daylight or under the night sky. You will find project ideas that look back to your tastes as a teenager and build a garden based on what you discover; you'll build a garden in a bowl, explore coastal gardening, and create a container garden that encourages you to look up more often, and after dark, and step into the world of miniature gardening. **V**

# Gardening with Your Thirteen-Year-Old Self

## PROJECT DESCRIPTION

I went back to my thirteen-year-old state of mind and created a gardening project using colorful tropical plants that I would have loved and enjoyed then, and certainly cherish today.

My thirteen-year-old self would love to have this sweet and slightly over-the-top trio of tropical plants in her room, starting with the bubblegum-pink plastic container.

For me, it was the late 1980s—a time of big hair, bright neon, and pastel colors; a lot of textured materials, leg warmers, and, of course, shoulder pads at any opportunity. As I remember, and gathered from photo albums, I was into flowers—a botanical preference that started in my childhood years. Wicker patio furniture was so in that I even managed to have a white loveseat in my small bedroom. Don't asked me how, but it fit.

Like many thirteen-year-olds, I was starting to push away from my parents' influence, to build my independence. I'm glad I didn't push too far. As a new teenager, I was copying styles I thought were cool from friends, television, movies, and magazines, and experimenting with fashion and hair styles while going through all the expected physical, emotional, and cognitive changes at that age.

To help me explore who I was becoming, my mother registered me in a refinement and modeling school. Every Saturday morning, from nine until noon, I would learn how to walk straight, and in heels, pose, and behave at a dinner table. I was learning about color palettes (for my makeup), the importance of contrasts, balance, and focal points, and how to style my big, curly hair. I'm fully convinced

Perla Sofía at thirteen, ready for her eighth grade graduation.

that part of my basic training in gardening started at thirteen.

This particular project was a fun, nostalgic activity. It required me to do some introspection, basic research, and take inventory of what I already have in my garden that could come in handy. The rest was like a scavenger hunt in garden centers—an adventure with a satisfactory outcome.

I ended up combining the dazzling foliage of a caladium (*Caladium*), a compacted wax begonia (*Begonia semperflorens*), and a sparkly gray artillery plant (*Pilea glaucophylla*) in a hot-pink container—a bold color that to this day, I really like playing with in the garden and as an accent color in my general décor.

I covered part of the leggy caladium stems with the compact begonia. Its numerous clusters of pink flowers with bright yellow centers

◁ Pretty in pink: From the container to the flowers and foliage, everyone here had their chance to be the center of attention.

Caladium foliage comes in a wide variety of colors and patterns—no two are alike, just as we were at thirteen. This white caladium with green veins and borders has irregular pink spots over its white areas.

Trimming the cascading red stems of the *P. glaucophylla* promotes a fluffy effect around the container and helps keep moisture in the soil for a longer period.

This particular begonia has massive clusters of flowers. Besides fuchsia, it comes in pale pink and white.

For watering, I use a straight nozzle and pour the water into the center of the container until the excess water drains out.

draw immediate attention to the mid part of the live arrangement.

To complete the trio, I added a patch of *P. glaucophylla* around both plants to cover the naked soil while creating a green, fluffy, padded effect within the container, just like some of the clothing I was wearing when I was thirteen: baggy pants and padded shoulders.

This rich combination of color and texture also has similar environmental requirements. Each plant can thrive indoors in bright indirect light, or outdoors in partial shade. The plants will thrive in temperatures of at least 60°F to 80°F (15.5°C to 27°C), with moist, well-drained soil.

The density of the plants' foliage in this particular container (plastic) will keep soil moist for a longer period.

This particular caladium foliage, semi-translucent white with small pink patches, green veins and edges, contrasts beautifully with the bronze-leaf begonia and the sparkly, red-stemmed gray *Pilea*. Certainly, this trio needed a brightly colored container that not only holds everything together but also complements each plant, giving each the opportunity to stand out.

Based on your thirteen-year-old self's taste, what plants and color palette would you choose?

## MAKE IT FUN AND PERSONAL

Are you excited to replicate this gardening concept? Understand that this project is meant to take time and provide fun during the process. You can compete it in a few days, depending on how much time you have and how deep you want to dig into your teenage years.

During the intel-gathering phase, start looking into your family photo albums; ask family members, or even childhood friends, what they remember about you when you were thirteen, or maybe of the time period. Validate or fact check your memories about trends, places, and social experiences. It's incredible how many trends from my teenage years I still embrace as an adult.

When you start choosing and putting together the materials for this project, you can start either with the container or the plants. Maybe the container you end up choosing represents a particular fashion in vogue around the time you were thirteen, or is a family heirloom passed down to you, or was your favorite color at that time.

Regarding the plants, choose them based either on their color palette, fragrance, or physical features that remind you of a particular experience at thirteen, or a person or interest you had then. Just remember that if you are combining them in the same container, they must share similar growing requirements to thrive.

Once assembled and completed, place your container in an accessible area where you can enjoy and admire it often, and when you feel like it, take the time to reflect on some of the lessons learned when you were thirteen and how they shaped you into the person you are today.

## Who Were You at 13?

To help you develop your concept and select plants and accessories, answer these questions:

1. What year did you turn thirteen?

   ---------------------------------------------------------------

2. Where did you live at that time?

   ---------------------------------------------------------------

3. What were your interests then?

   ---------------------------------------------------------------

   ---------------------------------------------------------------

   ---------------------------------------------------------------

4. Place a photo of yourself
   at thirteen here.

5. What were the color palette, plants, and other items on trend?

------------------------------------------------

------------------------------------------------

------------------------------------------------

------------------------------------------------

------------------------------------------------

------------------------------------------------

6. How would you describe your gardening project?

------------------------------------------------

------------------------------------------------

------------------------------------------------

------------------------------------------------

------------------------------------------------

------------------------------------------------

------------------------------------------------

## Materials used in this project

- One 5 × 11-inch (13 × 28 cm) medium-size fuchsia plastic bowl, with drainage holes
- Potting soil
- 1 fancy-leaf caladium with long petioles
- Hand spade
- Knife
- One 5-inch (13 cm) wax begonia with fuchsia flowers
- One 12- to 15-inch (30 to 37.5 cm)-long *Pilea glaucophylla* patch

## Preparing the container

1. Fill the container about three-fourths full with soil.
2. Place the caladium plant in the center of the container and cover its roots with soil.
3. Using a knife, divide the begonia in half through the roots and place the halves at each side of the caladium, covering part of the caladium's long petioles.
4. Place the *Pilea* around the container, right beneath the begonia and covering the naked soil.
5. Add more potting soil to the container, as needed.

# Wonder Bowl Garden

... LOOK AT THESE FOUND TREASURES! ...

## PROJECT DESCRIPTION

Right before the pandemic, we were already spending too much time indoors—at home, in the office, even in the car. The average person in the United States spends about 90 percent of their time indoors.

The little time spent outdoors is not enough to breathe in most of the benefits of fresh air, not to mention that this social phenomenon is keeping us away from enjoying the natural wonders that exist in our own backyard.

Reading about potential natural activities to motivate children and their families into going outside and playing more in the fresh air, I came across the simple idea of keeping a *wonder bowl* (or container) to place small natural things found while playing outside.

As I explored this concept more, I realized that I've been keeping my own wonder bowl my whole life; I just didn't have a name for it.

I think this a *WONDERful* activity to engage and explore nature at any age. And it is easy to do at home, school, or in the workplace. It promotes curiosity, social interaction, knowledge, and conservation, to mention a few potential benefits.

To elaborate, I created a green patched container garden within a terra-cotta bowl that can serve as a means to display any small curious natural objects found outdoors.

I used a few patches of angel's tears (*Soleirolia soleiroii*) as my only plant material for this project. I like its creeping growth habit, close to the soil, creating a soft natural green covering. You can propagate it by division, and it has so many practical uses in the garden. I've also used it to mulch around container plants and as a substitute for grass around flagstones.

◁ Patch the inside of a container with a creeping carpet-like plant and use it as a green display for natural found treasures.

In this case, once you place the plant at the bottom of your container, it will grow from there, expanding its stems up the sides, trying to reach the container's rim. I also patched a layer of soil to the inside wall of the container for the plant to attach to and grow stronger as it develops more roots. You can speed up this part by adding more patches, instead of waiting for the plant to expand by itself.

This is a project to be done in advance to have ready for the exploring and collecting activity.

When ready, place the bowl on an accessible table or countertop. Encourage the participants, depending on where the action is taking place, to touch the green mat and share some details about the plant.

Ask the participants to explore and collect small natural objects of interest—rocks, seeds, flowers, leaves, or empty snail shells—and display them on the carpet for others to observe and appreciate.

A third part of this experiential project could be spending time around the table

### About *Soleirolia soleiroii*

This beautiful plant, which blooms tiny blueish flowers, makes a lovely natural ground cover. You can use it to mulch around tiny trees, or in rock gardens, or around logs as an alternative to moss. The tiny green leaves grow tight and near the ground creating a carpeted look. You can propagate the plant by division. It grows best in temperatures of at least 34°F (1°C) to a maximum of 65°F (18°C). It thrives in humid shade or semi-shaded areas with well-drained soil. Keep it trimmed or deal with its invasive personality.

talking about what each person found and trying to figure out what the natural object is. This is a great opportunity to use and integrate technology into an outdoor activity. Also, you can use this particular project as a basis for nature journaling, asking participants to draw or write about the objects collected.

When finished, take all the objects out of the wonder bowl and, if necessary, return them to their original place. Bring your container garden to an area where it can continue to grow.

### Materials used in this project

- One 14-inch (35 cm) terra-cotta bowl
- Potting soil
- Hand spade
- Mister filled with water (optional)
- One 4-inch (10 cm)-square patch *Soleirolia soleiroii* (for alternative plants, see page 160)

### Preparing the container

1. Fill the container about halfway with potting soil.

2. Press the soil with your hands or fists from the bottom and up the sides, leaving 2 or 3 inches (5 or 7.5 cm) of soil in the bottom and a 1-inch (2.5 cm)-thick layer covering the container's walls.

3. Mist the potting soil, if you like, for better plant attachment.

4. Place the plant patch at the bottom of the container, or any of the inside areas covered with soil.

5. Cover the plant's roots with soil and water them to promote growth.

6. Before using it as a wonder bowl, place the container in a humid shaded or semi-shaded spot for a few weeks until you notice new growth, or the plant has covered the inside of the container completely.

7. To keep the carpeted look of the garden, trim any excess foliage creeping over the rim of your container, and remove any weeds growing in it.

# Coastal Garden

## PROJECT DESCRIPTION

According to the National Aeronautics and Space Administration (NASA), planet Earth has about 372,000 miles (620,000 km) of coastline. About 2.4 billion people in the world live within 60 miles (97 km) of an oceanic coast. I'm one of them.

Of the seventy-eight municipalities in Puerto Rico, forty-four have a coastline, defined as "the irregular boundaries between land and sea." My home is less than three miles (5 km) from the nearest beach.

All of my life I have lived and worked close to a blue space or visible water surface (river, lake, coastal water, canal). Although I don't consider myself a beach or watersport person, I do enjoy walking close to the shore and listening to the sound of the waves while observing the flora and fauna of the area.

Like other natural areas, blue spaces, too, provide restoration and contribute to reducing tension and depression symptoms as well as feelings of anger. Also, the access to and usage of these spaces promote physical health through activities such as swimming and other recreational sports, enhancing social connections.

A study with adults working in a beachfront building in Barcelona, Spain, found that when the participants walked four days a week, for at least twenty minutes, their general well-being and mood improved, with the positive effects lasting up to four hours.

In another study in New Zealand, researchers found that children visiting or living close to a beach experienced positive effects on their behavior and physical health. Even though limited, the evidence linking improved mental health with exposure to blue spaces keeps growing.

◁ Recreate a childhood memory using plants from a beloved blue space.

The vincas complement with a pop of color. I used Soiree Kawaii® (*Catharanthus roseus*), a compact variety.

Virginia, *Abuela Iña*, my father's mom, didn't have data to tell her how a walk on the beach would calm her grandkids when babysitting them. My grandmother lived right in front of a portion of the Atlantic Ocean, in a coastal neighborhood called Duhamel, in the municipality of Arecibo. My father, his three brothers, and his sister grew up there.

*Iña* would take us to the water as often as she could, and her body let her. To get there, we had to cross a street and a basketball court, then look for a safe path through a small rocky cliff to descend to the beach. We would hang onto the big rocks or any vegetation available, the kinds found mostly on sandy and rocky beaches on the coast.

My brothers, cousins, and I would run to the shore and then walk around looking for treasures buried in the sand or hidden between sharpened rocks. I would collect seashells, weird-looking rocks, and any other interesting objects. If the waves were too big, we would enjoy beach bathing in small natural pools—*pozas*—created by the waves inside the massive rocks. *Iña* would always scream at us to watch out for the stinging *erizos de mar* (sea urchins).

I also remember her front and backyard gardens. In her backyard, she had a few herbaceous plants, such as hibiscus, and a big sea

I placed the container over a patch of all-purpose sand for a more obvious beach look and to help the planter stand out from other container mixes in the garden.

almond tree (*Terminalia catappa*) that we liked to climb. The tree, native to Asia, can be used for timber and for artisanal wooden products, but extracting its fruit is complicated, so we used the fallen fruit to play dodgeball.

In the front yard, a raised bed made in cement was filled with vincas and ornamental asparagus to beautify the view from the living room. It was close to the balcony, the main gathering area, from which we could always see the infinite ocean.

I spent plenty of time in *Iña's* house, as a child and teenager. This coastal garden is a tribute to my childhood memories of those times in my grandmother's home. The plant mix aims to replicate what I saw growing in my *abuela's* garden and the neighborhood coast-line landscape.

The *Coccoloba uvifera*, seagrape, is an ideal tree for small places with moderate to slow growth. It's a native of Puerto Rico, and you see it everywhere near the coast as it loves sandy soil with good drainage. It attracts local birds, such as *Coeraba flaveola* (the bananaquit) and *Agelaius xanthomus* (the yellow-shouldered blackbird). As an ornamental, it's used for hedges, as well as to stand alone in the garden.

If you're using containers, start with the one that can provide enough space for the tree to develop strong, healthy roots. At its base, I placed two asparagus ferns (*Asparagus sprengeri* Regel) opposite one another, whose growing habit will help camouflage the bare tree stems.

For my coastal garden, I chose a sunny, breezy corner in the backyard. The container recipe is for a climate described as tropical marine, which is typically sunny, hot, and humid year-round, with temperatures between 76°F and 88°F (24°C and 31°C) in the coastal plains, and a humidity of 80 percent.

You can't miss it if you want to get to the meditation garden (see page 80). Because of its high exposure to sun and wind, this garden will need frequent watering, especially during the early stages of the tree's growth, but it is salt-tolerant and tolerant to dry areas as well.

## Materials used in this project

- Rake
- All-purpose sand
- One 15-gallon (57 L) plastic container with drainage holes
- Potting soil
- Hand spade
- One 3-gallon (11.4 L) seagrape tree (*Coccoloba uvifera*)
- Three 6-inch (15 cm) vincas, Soiree Kawaii® (*Catharanthus roseus*)
- Two 6-inch (15 cm) asparagus ferns (*Asparagus sprengeri* Regel)

## Preparing the space and container

1. Mark and clean the intended area for your container garden—from weeding to removing rocks.

2. Level the marked area using a rake and add more soil, if necessary.

3. Cover the area with sand, level and compact it, creating a nice-looking floor for your container.

4. Start your container in the designated area or a nearby location. Ask for help to move the container if it is too heavy for you.

5. Fill at least half of the container with potting soil and transplant your tree into the container. Make sure to cover all of its root ball with soil.

6. Place the asparagus ferns and the vincas around the tree, close to the container's rim, adding more soil to cover the plants' roots.

7. Water the plants until the container starts draining.

## FIVE DROUGHT- AND SALT-TOLERANT TREES AND SHRUBS FOR YOUR SUNNY COASTAL GARDEN

1. **Sea Buckthorn or Seaberry Plant** (*Hippophae rhamnoides*)
Woody shrub to small tree with thorny stems; deciduous; grows 8 to 12 feet (2.4 to 3.5 m) high; produces edible berries; used as a hedge, coastal windbreak, border, or screen; survives temperatures as low as -40°F (-40°C).

2. **Beach Plum** (*Prunus maritima*)
Shrub with white flowers; its fruit attracts birds and other wildlife; deciduous; grows up to 8 feet (2.4 m) high; used for dune restoration and landscaping; survives temperatures as low as -33°F (-36°C).

3. **Hawthorn** (*Crataegus crus-galli*)
Small flowering tree with thorns; deciduous; grows up to 35 feet (11 m) high; produces edible fruit; attracts birds and butterflies; used in landscaping as an ornamental tree; survives temperatures as low as -4°F (-20°C) when dormant.

4. **Smoke Tree** (*Cotinus coggygria*)
A small rounded tree with great visual interest; used in borders and groupings in landscaping; grows 10 to 15 feet (3 to 4.5 m) high; in summer, seed clusters turn a smoky pink color; in fall, leaves turn from blue-green to yellow-red-purple; survives temperatures as low as -20°F (-29°C).

5. **Bayberry** (*Myrica*)
Small deciduous rounded shrub; dense-branching; grows 6 to 10 feet (1.8 to 3 m) high; fragrant leaves; used in landscaping for erosion control, as informal hedging, and to screen and create borders; attracts birds; survives temperatures as low as -20°F (-29°C).

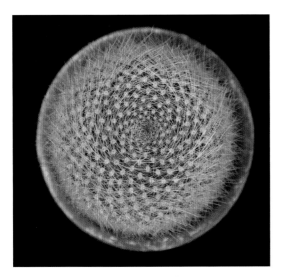

From above, the snowball cactus (*Mammilaria candida*) looks like one of Van Gogh's stars in his nightscape painting.

Cactus *Mammillaria elongata* in an aurora-inspired painted container.

## PROJECT DESCRIPTION

In 1963, the Arecibo Observatory was founded in Puerto Rico, property of the National Science Foundation (NSF), and eleven years later (I just gave away my age!) I was born in the same municipality. Coincidentally or not, that year, 1974, the first intentional message to extraterrestrials was transmitted from my hometown. According to information published on the observatory's website, the interstellar radio message, designed by Frank Drake in collaboration with Carl Sagan and others, carried "basic information about humanity and Earth."

As a kid, I visited this observatory two or three times, maybe as part of a school trip, summer camp, or a family excursion. This is certainly a landmark to visit when on the Island, and its contribution to science is invaluable. Through the years, the Arecibo Telescope has collected data on planets such as Mercury and Venus, information on Saturn's rings, and details on satellites, asteroids, and comets.

The night sky fascinates me as much as plants in the garden. Both scenarios can inspire us and make us question our purpose in life. But stargazing for inspiration is not as easy nowadays as it was for Vincent van Gogh when he created his famous painting *The Starry Night* while in Saint Rémy, France, in 1889.

Light pollution (inappropriate or excessive use of artificial light) has altered the way we experience the night environment, including in our own backyards. According to the International Dark-Sky Association (IDA), a third of the world's population can't see the Milky Way and 80 percent is affected by light pollution.

This type of contamination, which can be reversed, unlike others, affects our well-being, the climate, and the same wildlife we're trying to lure into our gardens. The excessive night glare blinds birds and confuses pollinators and other wildlife species about their essential roles in nature, such as mating, hunting, decomposing, reproducing in situ, and resting.

◁ Create and paint a night sky scene on terra-cotta containers and pair them with plants that look like they are out of this world.

To twinkle in a few facts, thanks to the natural night sky observations, we have been able to navigate the globe, learned the unimaginable about the Universe, and discovered that our flesh and blood have stardust, too.

If you live in an urban area like I do, you can probably appreciate only large stars, unless there is a blackout. However, this can be a great opportunity for you to start looking for ways to observe the night sky from your garden or community park and learn more about how the natural light quality in your area at night can affect your daylight experiences as well as the different flora and fauna species in your garden. This online statement from IDA, "The natural night sky is our common and universal heritage, yet it's rapidly becoming unknown to the newest generations," gave me even more cosmic inspiration for a gardening project here on Earth.

Aside from the moon and the stars, I like auroras. These glowing lights are described as the "scene-stealers of the winter sky" and are a night sky phenomenon seen generally in polar zones. According to an article published in *Explore the Night Sky* magazine, auroras are caused by charged particles from the sun interacting with Earth's magnetic field. When the particles reach lower altitudes "they hit and excite the gases in Earth's atmosphere, causing a distinctive colorful glow."

This is the glow I wanted to recreate on three terra-cotta containers using acrylic paint. For me, the easiest aurora pattern to paint, looking to the magazine's photos for inspiration, was the patch in which the appearance of the glowing lights has no particular shape. But you can try the arcs, rays, or corona patterns, or other galaxy designs as well.

This is a container garden that can be appreciated any time of day, in case your glow-in-the-dark paint doesn't work at night as expected. Also, I chose plants that reminded me somehow of the stars or complemented the container colors, while also considering the plants' requirements for survival here on Earth. Be aware that when painting terra-cotta pots, you take away their porosity and so plants will retain humidity for a longer period.

I chose succulent plants, such as the gold lace cactus (*Mammillaria elongata*) and snowball cactus (*Mammilaria candida*), each in its own pot, and took the adventurous road to combine a succulent (*Gasteraloe*) and a small conifer (*Juniperus procumbens*), also known as Japanese garden juniper, in a bowl. The 'Nana' cultivar (cold hardy to -30°F [-34°C]) is characterized by its slow-growing habit and prostrate branches that grow close to the soil.

Unless it's unsafe for your health and well-being, go outdoors at night, starting in your garden or a park nearby. Use this gardening project to ignite your curiosity to experience plants and local wildlife after dark, and remember to look up as much as possible.

## Reducing Light Pollution

To reduce light pollution coming from your home, and in your garden:

1. Minimize the light coming from your home at night.
2. Keep blinds drawn to keep light inside your home.
3. Use lighting only when and where needed.
4. For safety reasons, install motion-detector lights and timers.
5. Properly shield all outdoor lights.
6. Use dark-sky-friendly lighting to help minimize glare while reducing light trespass (light falling where it is not intended) and skyglow (a brightening of the night sky over inhabited areas).

Source: International Dark-Sky Association

## Materials used in this project

- Drop cloths
- 3 terra-cotta containers: 8-inch (20 cm), 7-inch (18 cm) low bowl, and 2¾-inch (7 cm), cleaned as needed
- Multi-surface acrylic paint in a dark blue
- Paint brushes
- Fluorescent acrylic paint in a light green
- Glow paint
- Potting soil for cacti and succulents
- Hand spade
- 2 cacti plants (such as *Mammillaria elongate* and *Mammilaria candida*)
- 1 succulent (such as *Gasteraloe* 'Flow')
- One 5-inch (13 cm) dwarf juniper (such as *Juniperus procumbens*)

Place the containers in a sunny spot where you can enjoy them together from a not-so-distant galaxy.

## Preparing the containers

1. Cover the area where you'll be painting with drop cloths.
2. Start painting your canvas by painting the containers using the dark blue paint. Let them dry completely. Use a picture to model your design.
3. Use the fluorescent light green paint to create swirls and movement in the auroral patches. Use several strokes to intensify the green color in different areas as you like. Let dry.
4. Brush on 1 or 2 layers of the glow paint and let dry under the sun to activate the glow effect of the paint. In a dark area, you will be able to see your container glowing.
5. Fill each dried container one-third full with the appropriate potting soil. If following exactly, use the largest container for the cacti, the medium-size container for the succulent with the juniper, and the smallest container for the snowball cactus.
6. Transplant the plants into their designated containers and cover their roots with soil.
7. Water the containers until they start to drain.
8. Place the container in a sunny spot outdoors, or in a room with bright indirect light.

## PROJECT DESCRIPTION

Miniature gardening is a fun and creative way to introduce *verdura* into your life. The purpose of a miniature garden's design is to tell a story through the combination of trees, herbaceous plants, hardscaping, and accessories used to create a themed landscaping design to enjoy indoors or outdoors, hopefully lasting more than one season.

Like bonsai, miniature gardens have their roots in East Asia design philosophy, specifically China, according to researcher Manuela Manda in the journal article "Miniature Landscapes." The bonsai refers to a dwarf potted tree (tray plant) pruned in an artistic way following formal rules; not to be confused with Hachi-Niwa, which are Japanese miniature gardens, or dish gardens.

As part of its evolution, Manda explains, "The miniature landscape takes different forms in the Western world from the [Asian] tradition—*pun-sai*, bonsai, *saikei* to modern variants, known as dish gardens, fairy gardens, and mini gardens, which can cover a wide range of consumer demands." The horticultural lecturer explained that the miniature Western gardens follow fewer rules and are built in simpler ways using a variety of containers and a handful of herbaceous plants, along with stones, mosses, and other decorative accessories.

Whether you have no garden space or limited time for a long list of gardening chores, creating a miniature garden offers a great opportunity to garden on a small scale.

Creating fairy gardens or teacup gardens, or building terrariums, as well as many other types of miniature gardens, can deliver numerous benefits, just as creating other regular gardens does. Through them, you can immerse

◁ Explore miniature landscaping using a meaningful item as the inspiration for your garden design.

**The BIG Benefits of Miniature Gardening**

- Improved self-esteem through a sense of accomplishment
- Lower stress levels as you slow your pace
- Improved sleep (light gardening is a form of exercise)
- Immediate transformation of your space
- Learning and growing

yourself into another world where, as opposed to virtual reality, you can touch and smell the elements. For me, working in a themed miniature garden gives me a sense of joy, adventure, and fantastical thrill.

As a kid (and still today), I loved how stores dressed up their windows during the holiday season. At the mall, some stores even decorated their entrances in such an inviting and magical way: using lights, stars, figurines, even a small train circling the different holiday scenes, anything to catch your attention, and, of course, your parents' wallets, to entice you into the store.

I have only a vague memory of the miniature make-believe landscapes, but what I do remember vividly is the joyful feeling I had while watching these mesmerizing window displays. I imagined myself immersed in the

For the benefit of our imaginary tenants, it is important to plant "shade trees" as well as "bushes" and hedges to provide cool outdoor spaces that attract more wildlife and invite us to enjoy the outdoors, with a good book and a cup of coffee.

For this project, I used a wooden figurine as the focal point of the miniature garden.

scenes, and then, at night, dreamed about what I saw, creating my own story. I guess this is what I look forward to every time I build a miniature garden: recreating a lost feeling while tapping into my fantastical imagination.

The principles applied in miniature gardening are similar to the ones we use in regular garden design: balance, shape, texture, color, and focus. The focal point in a miniature garden can be a color, plant, or accessory, but the most important thing is maintaining the proportions when selecting the plants, pots, and other features.

Many parents use this kind of project as an opportunity to bond with their kids, but this is also a garden-*tainment* experience you can share with coworkers during a team-building exercise. Putting together a miniature garden project requires working with limitations and other challenges (space, small botanical specimens, environmental factors) that need solutions using the imagination in more creative ways—skills applicable in any workplace.

For this project, I created a miniature garden using a wooden bookstore figurine as the focal point. I found the collector's item in a thrift store and immediately knew that I wanted to create a scene, as if it were part of a small town, like those on the Hallmark Channel.

Like any business that wants to continue attracting customers, it is important to keep entrances accessible, clean, and illuminated when the sun goes down, reflecting the spirit of well-being that could be experienced easily in other parts of the little town.

Once you activate your imagination, you'll continue adding elements, creating a story and looking for a way to recreate it.

To make the planting process easier, I like to sketch the type of garden I have in mind on a piece of paper. Nothing formal. This serves as a guide, especially when I am looking for plants with specific characteristics. With a drawing, you also realize that bringing your scene to life might require adjustments and edits, something done more easily on paper than in the actual container.

## Materials used in this project

- Hand spade
- Potting soil
- One 8 × 5½ × 1½-inch (20 × 14 × 3 cm) terra-cotta tray with drainage
- One 4 × 5-inch (10 × 13 cm) wooden accessory (your focal-point element)
- Herbaceous plants (the final amount will depend on the size of your container; make sure all the plants share similar growing requirements):
  » 1 "tree" (such as asparagus fern [*Asparagus setaceus*], or other small plant or special variety that will function as a tree)
  » "Shrubs" (such as foxtail fern [*Asparagus densiflorus*], or other small plants or special varieties that will function as shrubs and bushes)
  » "Vines" (such as sedums and ivy plants [*Hedera helix*], or other small plants or special varieties that will function as a vine)
  » "Ground covers" (small plants or special varieties that will function as ground cover)
- ¼-inch (6 mm) or smaller pea gravel
- Variety of miniature accessories (figurines, lamps, trash cans, fences, seats, tables)
- Water dropper
- Plant stand (optional)

## Preparing the container

1. Place a thin layer of soil in the terra-cotta container and place the focal piece where you'd like it. Mark the area, then remove the item.

2. In one corner of the container, plant the "tree" and other small "shrubs" and cover their roots with soil.

3. In another corner of the container, plant more "shrubs" and "vines."

4. Replace the focal point in the area you marked.

5. Create a gravel path.

6. Add the rest of the details of your story using the accessories you've selected.

7. To hydrate the plants, use a water dropper.

8. Place the project on a plant stand indoors, if you like, where it will receive indirect bright light.

# Be Social

Gardening and garden-based activities are excellent opportunities to entertain yourself and others.

EVEN THOUGH YOU can derive so many direct benefits from nature alone, interacting with others through green experiences has even greater outcomes.

Before the pandemic, I coordinated monthly in-person gardening workshops, and after each one, attendees completed an evaluation form, which included stating the reason they attended the session. Every time, the number-one reason was to socialize.

Attendees of all ages, some of them frequent guests, wanted to learn in the company of others and compare gardening experiences while enjoying a coffee or hot chocolate, relaxing, or cultivating new friendships.

Being involved in any activity around plants gives you a healthy platform to connect with others with similar interests, alleviate loneliness, and satisfy your need for belonging, even virtually. Also, any gardening project shared with another person or group has the potential to enhance your mental health so you experience more positive emotions and look forward to making more plans for the future, increasing your chances of living a long, healthy life.

When in a new place or trying to meet others in your neighborhood, participating in a community garden or creating a garden of your own, on a balcony or in a front yard, gives you a social push.

I tend to perceive people who love plants and gardens as friendlier. Even if you feel shy to make the first move, others might feel comfortable asking you anything plant-related, and so it begins.

For me, gardening has been one of the main topics I share with my neighbors. You guessed it—I have a lot of plants on my balcony alone. We talk about flowers, houseplants, garden tools, where to buy the best soil, and, of course, what is wrong with my plants, too.

In my backyard, I share a Rangoon creeper vine (*Combretum indicum*) with my next-door neighbors—a gift from one frequent attendee of my then-gardening workshops. Now, I get to share it with others.

It makes me so happy to be near people who enjoy nature as much as I do. Instead of complaining about branches creeping on their side of the fence, my neighbors expressed gratitude about how they have been enjoying the flowering vines, the continuous bird tweeting, and the cooling effects of having this plant shading their backyard terrace. They, too, have filled their balcony with all sorts of flowering plants.

But not all people will enjoy gardening or nature the same way or as much as you do, and that is okay. Back when I was growing up, I remember a couple of neighbors on my street complaining to my mother about having to rake leaves that they swore were coming exclusively from our front-yard tree (*Tabebuia rosea*). Some even had the audacity to suggest cutting down the tree. Of course, it never happened, and, eventually, the heated arguments went away, just as the leaves flew by the wind.

The next group of *verduras* will inspire you to connect one on one, share your gratitude with friends and family (including those who enjoy greenery in small doses), and, maybe, speed up that garden spot at home, right on time to throw a small get-together and share the fruits and the added value of your labor, literally. **v**

## Self-Assessment Time

Do a self-assessment to help you increase your social connection a bit more by answering these questions.

1. Do you prefer gardening by yourself or having a garden buddy?

   ----------------------------------------

2. How would you describe your ideal garden buddy?

   ----------------------------------------

   ----------------------------------------

3. What kind of gardening activities would you rather do by yourself?

   ----------------------------------------

   ----------------------------------------

4. What kind of gardening activities would you rather do with others?

   ----------------------------------------

   ----------------------------------------

5. When you have a plant question, who would you ask first: A friend or Google?

   ----------------------------------------

   ----------------------------------------

6. Which of your friends would you have the most fun with at a garden party? Why?

   ----------------------------------------

   ----------------------------------------

   ----------------------------------------

# Hanging Planter Duo

## PROJECT DESCRIPTION

My husband knows that my almost-daily garden-related activities are a win-win for us both. Gardening is not his favorite thing, but he enjoys the results that come from me doing it. He loves the plants that I put around the house, especially in his home office, and we talk from time to time about their care.

On occasion, he joins me at the garden center or on a treasure hunt in secondhand stores to share my passions, as I do with him. We hold each other dear, getting to know each other even better.

As gardening has helped me become a better person, it also has helped me be a better partner. Since I became an active gardener, I am more relaxed, creative, generous, and civil, and I bring all of these qualities to my marriage.

Sharing hobbies or activities, such as gardening, with your partner has been proven to strengthen the relationship because, in the process, you nourish your relationship with more conversation, building trust and respect.

Of course, this applies to friendships, too. When we go plant shopping with a friend, ask for their help with a gardening project, or exchange garden advice, that also contributes to bringing us closer and making the time together more enjoyable. You may even feel more comfortable opening up about other subjects you might not normally discuss in another situation.

When you develop this type of strong bond through gardening, whether with your romantic partner or a garden buddy, you will experience instances where you feel you have found a match made in heaven. Not only will

◁ Hang a couple of matching plants in a bright spot. Ask your partner or a friend to help you in the process.

you want to hang out with that other person as much as possible, but you will also know you can trust them. Even if disagreements come up—trust me, they will—you know you're going to make it through.

Turn this next gardening project into a fun partnership exercise. Ask your gardening partner to play along, especially if you don't live together. Let's see how much you know and trust each other!

For a long time, I wanted to hang a couple of plants from my home office curtain rod. Thanks to the big glass windows, the room is always well lit, which keeps the houseplants happy and healthy. Although the rod is secured to the walls, it won't hold too many, or heavy, plants on it. Even less desirable would be hanging plants there whose eventual growth would interfere with the light for the rest of the plants in the room. So, finding the right match wasn't limited to the window area, but to the plants and containers, too.

I found two matching ceramic pots in a secondhand store, hand-painted and made in Italy. Gorgeous. They were the perfect size and meant to be shown off, meaning that the plant to be selected for each container couldn't cover them. I decided on a mini monstera (*Rhaphidophora tetrasperma*) that I propagated, and a Swiss cheese plant (*Monstera adansonii*) that I purchased in a garden center. They weren't the same plant but they look alike and share similar light and humidity requirements. Also, when hanging, their stems grow into a spilling pattern.

I invite you to share a similar hanging planter project with your gardening partner. You can either do everything together (from selecting the plants, the containers, the gardening, and the hanging) or trust each other and divide the tasks.

If you go for the latter, once the hanging location details are identified, set the budget for the plants, containers, and any other accessories, and decide who's going to pick and buy what (you pick the containers, and your friend the plants, or vice versa). Set a date to meet with all the needed materials and make it a garden gathering for two. This fun adventure with your partner or friend will not only bring you closer but will also give you meaningful laughs and conversations.

When you are done with the project, and everyone continues with their routine, every time you care for the hanging planter, you will be reminded of and appreciate the relationship you have built, adding joyful memories to your life experience list.

## Materials used in this project

- Two 5-inch (13 cm) plants, such as mini monstera (*Rhaphidophora tetrasperma*) and Swiss cheese plant (*Monstera adansonii*)
- Two 7-inch (18 cm) vintage, or other decorative, ceramic containers with no drainage holes
- Two 25-inch (62.5 cm)-long macramé hangers
- Potting soil
- Hand spade
- Mulch (optional)

## Preparing the container

1. Water the plants and let them drain.
2. Place each plant, still in its plastic garden pot, into a ceramic pot. If either of the plants is too big for the ceramic pot or too heavy for hanging, divide it and plant just half using the potting soil to fill the rest of the ceramic pot.
3. Hang the macramé holders from a secured curtain rod and then add and adjust the ceramic containers with the plants.
4. When caring for the plants, if necessary, remove the macramé hangers and place them on a secure and flat surface.

# A Garden Gathering at Home

## PROJECT DESCRIPTION

When I started working in my garden spaces, back and front, I kept picturing myself using the spaces for growing all sorts of plants, but also for activities such as meditating, reading, and taking quick garden breaks. I added the sitting areas and—guess what?—that's how I mostly used my garden.

However, if I want to bring some friends over or have a small family gathering, guess where we meet? Exactly, indoors, because the garden space I was working so hard to transform didn't have specific areas that would allow it to be used that way. So, I decided to add a loveseat and a secondhand bistro set to the backyard patio that would encourage more social interaction (other than my husband's) outdoors.

Our gardens, no matter the size or location, are spaces that offer the opportunity for reconnecting with nature as well as with friends and family. Having a conversation, even a serious one, under the shade of a tree or near a fragrant bed of roses eases any circumstances. Our guard is down, and we tend to pay more attention to the content of the conversation, even giving better feedback, while enjoying the physical benefits of fresher air and all sort of natural stimuli.

If garden gatherings are something you want to increase in your social agenda, start planning for them. The meet-up can be as big as your garden space can hold or just you and someone else.

Gatherer expert Priya Parker explains that a gathering is "the conscious bringing together of people for a reason," and they "shape the way we think, feel, and make sense of our

◁ Set up your garden space and challenge yourself to plan a special meet-up to enjoy with others.

world." In her book *The Art of Gathering: How We Meet and Why It Matters*, Parker suggests that if we want to have meaningful and enjoyable encounters, with friends and family, we should start by understanding the real reasons we choose to gather. "When we don't examine the deeper assumptions behind why we gather, we end up skipping too quickly to replicating old, staid formats of gathering. And we forgo the possibility of creating something memorable, even transformative."

Let's start by doing just that—going beyond the generic reasons for inviting someone, or a group of people, over to our precious green spaces. Consider this a challenge more than a gardening project, although you will probably need to do some gardening for your patio events.

Start by strengthening your gathering skills by organizing a small reunion for one or two people. Take your time and think about your friends, and about why you would invite that person to your garden. Is it to cheer a friend going through a tough personal moment? Or, do you want to celebrate and laugh so hard with a couple friends you haven't seen in a long time?

The same garden space that we take care of every day can become a space of solace as well as entertaining and uplifting others. And, if cheering up someone is the outcome you're looking for, for example, your real purpose, as Parker calls it in her book, will lead the rest of your planning.

Here, I share some of the things I did in my backyard before inviting a friend over, as well as other important tasks that will make your process easier regardless of the size of your reunion.

The purpose of my micro-gathering, let's just say, was to catch up with each other after a grueling year. Definitely, the desired outcome was to relax and celebrate our endurance.

You can use each of the following areas as a checklist for planning and organizing your small garden gathering. Of course, if you're looking to organize something bigger and formal, by all means, hire a specialist.

After your garden gathering, send a thank-you note to your guest(s) via email, or continue the memorable experience by sending a handwritten note. (See "Say it with *Verdura!*", page 56, for more ideas.)

## Planning and Organizing Your Gathering Space

**Purpose of the gathering:** Decide why you want to meet.

**Budget:** Establish how much money you can spend. Exceeding your budget can create stress and anxiety.

**Guest(s):** Based on the purpose of your gathering and budget, prioritize who you want to come to your event, unless is just you and someone else.

**Invitations:** Whether you call, send an email, or post via a carrier, alert your guests a few weeks ahead to the day of the event, including basic details like time, location, and dress code as well as the purpose of the occasion. Ask for confirmation of attendance within a reasonable time frame.

**Location:** Even if you're hosting in your garden, select the specific area where you're planning to host. Will you need an umbrella or a tent in case of rain? Is it easily accessible or complicated to get there?

**Decoration:** Depending on the specific location, your guests, and the purpose of the gathering, you can decide on the type of furniture needed, theme, accessories, and other details regarding the event. Make sure to integrate specific elements of your garden, such as cut flowers or table wreaths, into the decorations.

**Food and Drink:** The refreshments you'll serve will be based on the purpose of the gathering, your guests (ask for food allergies and/or preferences with their invitation acceptance), and your budget.

**Entertainment:** Curate a playlist to set the mood and choose activities that promote inclusion and the active participation of all guests.

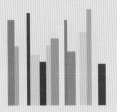

# Little Library
# Garden

## PROJECT DESCRIPTION

I grew up in a three-bedroom suburban home with two bathrooms and well-defined areas for the kitchen, living room, and dining room. We had a backyard to play in and a garage space for two cars. It was a comfortable house for our family of five and still is for my parents, who have lived there for more than fifty years.

We had books everywhere. Both my parents are avid readers and so my brothers and I always saw them reading something, whether the newspaper, a classic, or the latest bestseller. We did not have a library or extra room to store all those books, as you would see on television or in the movies, but we did have an extra closet.

The "library closet" was located right in the center of the house. You could have easy access to it as soon as you stepped out of your room. The encyclopedia collection was kept on the top shelves, followed by all of my parents' novels, poetry, and essay books and, of course, all the dictionaries, the thesaurus, children's books, and some school textbooks ended up there, too.

Sometimes we had to make space on certain shelves for towels, shampoo, and soap. This was until, a few years later, my father built his home office in the backyard, where he then moved all the books to give them their proper space.

It's not a surprise, then, that I became an avid reader, wanting my own private library filled with my favorite books.

Reading is still one of my favorite things to do, especially in the garden when I'm not gardening. Most of the time I read gardening books, but I enjoy all sorts of topics and categories—from business and human behavior to suspense and romance novels. There is no doubt that my love for books started early with my parents' example.

It has been well documented that children who have early access to books do better in school, develop better writing skills, and have better vocabularies and abundant imaginations, with a higher probability of reading more books as adults.

Recent studies have suggested that children under the age of eight who have access to books and adult support or influence in choosing their reading materials tend to do better in literacy development.

Unfortunately, not all kids have books at home or enough quality reading options at school, or even a public library nearby. This is why I love concepts like the Little Free Library, a nonprofit organization in the United States that promotes book access in communities, meeting kids and their families where they are.

Since it started in 2009, the book sharing program has grown into more than 150,000 libraries (even mobile) and registered Little Free Libraries in 110 countries, according to their website. I first learned about the program while touring gardens in Buffalo, New York, and fell in love with it immediately.

For obvious reasons, one of the many design ideas I'm drawn to is having a garden around or near the little libraries, beautifying and attracting even more attention to the area. Cicero said it best: "If you have a garden and a library, you have everything you need." So, I asked my friend and home improvement specialist Carly Carrión, who also happens to also be an engineer, to build a small bookcase for me to insert into a bigger container filled with flowering plants.

This is definitely a creative and fun project to do with family and friends. This is something you can steward for your community or you can build in your backyard to encourage your children to read while outdoors.

Before the building process started, Carly and I discussed who would use the library, its location, and its functional design. In my case,

◁ Build and insert a bookcase in a garden container.

My friend Carly cut the treated wooden panels to the right measurements.

The wooden library, ready to be painted, opens from the top like a tailgate. You will be able to see its contents through the opening, covered with an acrylic sheet.

I wanted to have a mobile library that I could place in the front garden during special occasions, protected behind the balcony as I live in a walk-up building, and fill it with reading materials that could be of interest to my neighbors. Once we had a plan, we set a date, bought the materials, and built the little bookcase for my front yard garden.

I later painted it a bright-yellow color and surrounded its base with two plants that my mother used to keep around the house: yellow portulacas (*Portulaca grandiflora*) and golden trumpet (*Allamanda cathartica*). This is a hard-to-miss library!

When placing the little library garden for public use, share a simple explanation of the project and some ground rules regarding the books as well as the plants in the container. Add books you've already read and think others might like and include books for kids and for those interested in gardening.

**You can divide this kind of project into three phases**

1. Buying the construction materials, paint supplies, and plants
2. Building and painting the little library
3. Preparing the container garden and adding the library

Once the plants were incorporated, I patted the soil to compact it where the base of the wooden library will rest.

## Materials used in this project

### FOR BUILDING THE LITTLE BOOKCASE

- Handsaw
- Two 17-inch high (at the back) × 15-inch high (at the front) × 11-inch wide (43 × 37.5 × 28 cm) treated wood planks for the side panels. Each panel should be cut with the top angled so the back is 2 inches (5 cm) taller than the front. This supports a sloped roof
- One 17-inch high × 15-inch wide (43 × 37.5 cm) treated wood plank for the back side panel
- One 11-inch high × 14-inch wide (28 × 35.5 cm) treated wood plank for the bottom panel
- One 13-inch high × 15-inch wide (33 × 37.5 cm) treated wood plank for the top roof panel
- One 15-inch wide × 11½ inch high (37.5 × 29.2 cm) treated wood panel for the door
- One 12-inch wide × 8-inch high (30.5 × 20.3 cm) acrylic sheet to make a window in the bookcase door
- Sandpaper
- Scissors
- Wood glue
- Hammer and 32 nails
- Screwdriver and 4 wood screws
- Two 2-inch (5 cm) hinges
- Yellow latex paint
- Paintbrush
- 1 hook-and-eye-latch to hold the library's door closed
- Piece of impermeable liner, such as a pond liner or rubber sheeting (optional)
- Staple gun with staples
- Books to fill the library

### FOR THE CONTAINER GARDEN

- One 23 × 17-inch (58 × 43 cm) plastic terra-cotta-colored container
- 1 rolling plant caddy (optional)
- Mulch
- Potting soil
- Hand spade
- One 5-inch (13 cm) yellow golden trumpet (*Allamanda cathartica*) plant
- Three 5-inch (13 cm) yellow portulaca (*Portulaca grandiflora*) plants

## Preparing the bookcase

*Note:* For direction and design inspiration, we checked various links recommended on the Little Free Library website (littlefreelibrary.org) and made adjustments to meet our needs—from purpose and budget to accessibility issues. Eventually, you can add other accessories or decorative elements to your wooden structure.

1. Ensure all wood planks are cut to the desired measurements. Sand all the cut edges.
2. Cut an opening in the bookcase door at your preferred size. This will become the window (the one shown in the photo is 8 × 9 inches [20 × 23 cm]). Cut the acrylic sheet 1 inch (2.5 cm) wider and 1 inch (2.5 cm) longer than the opening's width and length (this is so the acrylic sheet will overlap the wood ½ inch [1 cm] on all sides). Secure the acrylic sheet to the door panel from the inside using four screws.
3. Apply wood glue to the end edges of the back plank. One by one, line up each side plank to the back plank and push together so the glue sticks. Then hammer the back and side together using nails. Repeat with the other side.

4. Attach the back and sides to the bottom plank. Place the angled side of the boards onto a flat surface so that the bottom is up in the air. Apply glue all along the bottom edge and then place the bottom plank on top, securing it in place with hammer and nails. Flip the box so that the bottom is on the flat surface and repeat the gluing and hammering with the roof panel.
5. Attach the hinges to the front of the bottom panel and to the bottom edge of the door panel so the door opens from the top like a tailgate.
6. Paint the bookcase and let it dry. Once dry, add the hook-and-eye latch at the top of the door panel to hold it closed.
7. You can add an impermeable liner to the interior of the bookcase to prevent water leaks in case of heavy rain. Cut the liner material large enough to cover the inside of the top, bottom, and side panels. Secure the liner to the planks with a staple gun and cut off the excess.

## Preparing the container

1. Wash the container with soap and water to reduce the chances of passing potential pests to your new plants and let dry.
2. To help make the container easier to move around, you can place a rolling plant caddy (if using) under the container. To keep it lighter to move, fill the container first about half full with mulch. Top the mulch with potting soil.
3. Transplant the golden trumpet and portulacas into the container near the rim. The golden trumpet will grow as a small bush with filler tendency and the portulacas will grow and spill over the container's edge. Water profusely.
4. Level the top of the soil where the bookcase will sit and place the bookcase on it.
5. Add your books.

# Bring Your Herb Cocktail and Mocktail Garden Bar Anywhere

Grow your favorite herbs in small containers for mixing into drinks and place them on a cart to move them around easily.

## PROJECT DESCRIPTION

Something magical happens when passing plants around a room, especially if they are aromatic herbs. People touch and rub the leaves, dive their noses into them, even dare to snip a tip to taste, and giggle or comment immediately to the closest person, whether a friend or a total stranger. Plants are natural icebreakers.

That is a ritual I love to practice during in-person workshops, and even virtually. I watch people's reactions during this brief encounter, a prelude to the next part: the project.

Moments like this are small windows for opportunities to get to know other people, if only we pay attention. Herbs are great for stimulating all of our senses. During this close interaction with the plant, we share, simply by our reaction, whether we like what we see, touch, smell, or taste. We search our memory as to whether we have that plant in our garden currently, or have interacted with it at a certain point in our lives, or simply become mesmerized by the new information we just acquired.

As soon as we unlock our memories, we feel compelled to tell someone else, about the good or the bad experiences, the validation about the plant choice, or the excitement for what is about to come.

What would happen if we used plants in our social gatherings more often and consciously? At home, the workplace, or at a party. As scientific studies have validated constantly, plants boost moods, help reduce stress, and contribute to feelings of happiness. For sure, I want to be around and engage more with people while feeling less stressed and more enthusiastic.

Herbs are great additions to our gardens, and if you're looking to embrace your gardening lifestyle, they are the best plants to start with.

A huge variety of herbs can grow in almost any small, sunny spot. They don't need a great amount of soil depth and grow faster than many

Herbs also are star ingredients in some of most our beloved drinks, from iced and hot teas to cocktails and nonalcoholic mocktails. You can also create herbal infusions or special syrups that go into recipes.

other plants. They can excite us to cook more and expand our curiosity about other new cultivars. They even make our lives smell better.

You can turn this next project into a social experiment, whether at home or as part of a team-building experience for colleagues at the office.

Create a mobile herb garden bar for easy transportation and interaction. Whether you use a rolling cart, a garden station on a caddy, or single potted plants that you carry yourself from one place to another, they will need a sunny spot to grow, hydrated soil, fertilizing, and regular trimming to promote growth.

Before putting your herb bar together, ask people (family members, colleagues, friends) about their favorite drinks. Then, do a little research about which herbs are essential in those drinks, or that might enhance them. Choose herbs that can be used in several drink recipes (alcoholic and nonalcoholic), such as basil, mint, or rosemary. Get acquainted with how to grow them, each plant's needs, and

whether some can share the same container to maximize space, or need their own space to grow.

When planning this project as part of a work event, check company policies regarding plants, for any type of consumption or interaction. Remember, some plants can cause allergic or toxic reactions in people when used individually or in any type of recipe.

If you are an adult who likes cocktailing or hosting gatherings involving alcoholic drinks, match your herb garden to some of your favorite spirits' profiles. Creating a themed garden is always fun and adds another interesting layer to our social conversations. For example, create a rum or vodka garden featuring herbs that are used or that enhance well-known recipes incorporating that spirit.

## Materials used for this project

- 1 three-level rolling cart
- Several fresh herbs (such as basil, lavender, marjoram, mint, and rosemary) planted in terra-cotta containers or pots of different shapes and sizes
- Removable adhesive labels or plant tags

## Preparing the container

1. Place your selected plants in a sunny location to grow bigger and healthier before using them in any project.

2. Identify the potted plants using labels or tags. You can include the common name or its botanical one. If you have more space, add other interesting details.

3. Gather your drink ingredients, such as spirits, syrups, and infusions, as well as important ingredients to recipes, like ice, sugar, salt, and spices.

4. When is time to use the herbs for your gathering, transfer them to the rolling cart and bring them inside.

5. Before preparing any beverages, pass the herbs around or hand them to your guests or family members. Share any details you know about the herb and encourage others to touch, rub, and smell the leaves. If you are using the herbs for a drink, let them know that, too.

6. If necessary, take the plants out of the cart and place them in a visible and accessible location for people's further interactions. Leave written notes close by with handling instructions.

## Favorite Spirits and Herbs to Match

Gin ........................basil, lemongrass, thyme

Rum .....................basil, ginger, mint, rosemary

Tequila ................lemongrass, mint, rosemary

Vodka...................basil, ginger, mint, rosemary, thyme

Whiskey..............rosemary

# Say It with Verdura!

## PROJECT DESCRIPTION

Use some of your garden breaks to write and send thank-you cards. It will have a positive impact on your well-being and on the receiver's as well. According to research, expressing our gratitude to others can make us feel good and also promote feelings of happiness and excitement in other people.

A few years ago, I sent a thank-you card to a communications executive from a well-known nonprofit organization in Puerto Rico after having met at a public event. I had a wonderful chat with this person and, the next day, I sent her the handwritten note.

Sometimes, thank-you emails "get lost" or missed in our digital inboxes, but receiving an unexpected package or card in the mail is like opening a present. You stop whatever you're doing and pay attention to its content.

A month later, I was sitting in her office discussing communications projects. We collaborated for almost two years, and she remains a good friend today. I'm glad I decided to express my gratitude without overthinking what her reaction might be.

Doing this made me feel good and grateful for the opportunity to meet important and interesting people in my field, but also my self-esteem got a boost of confidence when I received a thank-you email for the gesture of handwriting a note.

My manners surprised and impressed the other person and helped transform our first social encounter into a new relationship that affected my personal and professional life in a positive way.

In the journal article "Undervaluing Gratitude: Expressers Misunderstand the Consequences of Showing Appreciation,"

◁ Decorate a thank-you note with pressed flowers and other botanicals to boost and strengthen your social connections.

Adding botanical materials, like flowers and leaves, makes the sentiment even more special and personal, especially if those materials come from your garden.

researchers Kumar and Epley found that not being aware of the positive effects that expressing our gratitude has on others gets in the way of people sending more gratitude letters.

They also found that people overestimated the receiver's reaction—from *they already know how grateful I'm* to *if I send a gratitude note it's not a big deal for the other person* to overthinking feelings of being judged, or scrutinized, because of the note's content.

On the contrary, the research showed that people who receive gratitude notes felt "ecstatic," instead of awkward, as the majority of senders believed.

Even in the workplace, a thank-you note from managers to their team members can boost morale, performance, and loyalty toward the organization.

In a *Harvard Business Review* article, authors O'Flaherty et al., said that gratitude notes, along with certificates and public recognition, are symbolic awards that can be used strategically to support people when money-based awards are not an immediate option. According to the authors, personalized gratitude cards can positively reduce employee turnover, too. The authors shared that people reported feelings of appreciation and support after knowing that a leader, or someone they look up to, took the time to make something special for them. An appreciation letter, sent either publicly or privately, can do wonders for the person's well-being as well as for the business.

Knowing now of all the great good a small note can do for you and for others, it makes it worth the time to sit down and prepare a list of all the people you would like to say "thank you" to.

This project is cost-effective and customizable with unimaginable rewards.

If you're the kind of person who worries about your words and writing style being scrutinized, the natural elements on this beautifully embellished thank-you note can divert the focus from the written content. This is a project you can divide into several tasks over a period of time before putting it together and getting it ready to post.

## Materials used in this project

- A few 5 × 8-inch (13 × 20 cm) blank note cards with envelopes
- Dried, pressed flowers and other botanical materials (such as flower heads, small seeds, and leaves; buy them already pressed online or press your own, see step 2 below)
- Glue stick
- Ruler and scissors (optional)

## Preparing the note cards

1. Gather your list of note card recipients and their addresses.

2. Gather the botanical materials you'll use. If pressing your own, place the items between sheets of absorbent paper and place the paper on a hard surface. Place the heaviest book you can find on top for a couple of weeks until the botanicals are dried enough to use.

3. Meanwhile, plan the card's layout: Where will you write your message (center, left, or right side)? Where will you place the botanicals? Will you write the note first, or attach the pressed flowers?

4. If writing the note first, do that, including a personal detail or short comment about the botanical materials used for the card, and address and stamp the envelope while you're waiting for the botanicals to dry. When the flowers are ready, glue them to the card and let dry completely before inserting the card into the addressed envelope.

5. Drop the cards in the mail and feel good about the joy you're spreading.

# Encourage Wellness

For many years, I was writing and talking about gardening and its benefits but not necessarily practicing what I encouraged.

YES, I WAS ATTENDING many horticultural events, farmers' markets, and even tending plants at home. However, I was treating plants and gardens as another topic to cover while stressing about everything else—from finances and personal relationships to career choices to name a few.

While conducting one of my many rabbit-hole online inquiries for an article I was writing, I stumbled upon the topic of horticulture therapy (HT)—the use of plants and gardens, by a trained professional, for the well-being of people with defined and clinically documented goals and outcomes. (A therapeutic horticulture program follows the same principles, but the goals and outcomes for the participants are not within a clinical context). Immediately, I was hooked.

This new well of information combined knowledge in human behavior, which resonated with me and my major in psychology; horticulture, great, I was already working as a specialized journalist in the field; and best of all, people in HT were creative, strategic communicators and wellness promoters. I knew what I needed to do.

I began immersing myself in the gardening process, questioning how the things I wanted to do in my garden could help me feel less stressed and more empowered to accomplish other endeavors. As I started noticing better results, it was clear to me that gardening needed to be part of my daily routine. You can't promote gardening for wellness unless you consciously experience its benefits for yourself.

Years later, I ended up completing a horticulture therapy certification and changing my drive and the purpose of my business: to help people connect the joy, fun, and benefits of gardening (no matter the type or size of the project) to their particular needs.

Today, I use my garden space for daily check-ups on my mental health. I take garden breaks more often and, as you have probably noticed by now, I feel pretty confident in using it for work-related projects, too.

Speaking of which, the next group of gardening projects is meant for stimulating our senses more consciously. One of the greatest benefits of gardening is that it gives us the opportunity to use more than one sense at the same time. Not only do we collect more information about the world we're in, but we also increase our chances of living a healthier life.

From creating a garden space for growth and meditation, container gardens to taste and enjoy the scent or touch of plants, particularly with bare feet, to transforming the immediate view, even if the bigger picture is uncontrollable, these fun activities can be adjusted easily to your location and mood.

Stress and anxiety are still part of my life, but I can manage them better within my garden. I gather myself and refocus faster, applying many of the strategies I've learned along the way, and I'm happy to encourage others to garden for their wellness. **V**

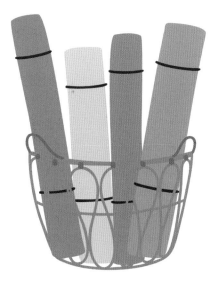

## Self-Assessment Time

Do a self-assessment to help you be more aware of the things that encourage your well-being by answering these questions.

1.  What do you usually do when feeling stressed?

    --------------------------------------------------

    --------------------------------------------------

2.  What kind of things do you enjoy doing in the garden or public green space that make you smile and feel relaxed? Mention three.

    --------------------------------------------------

    --------------------------------------------------

3.  List, in order of preference, areas at your home (or work) you like to spend time in.

    --------------------------------------------------

    --------------------------------------------------

4.  List three or more plants that you associate with happy and tasty memories.

    --------------------------------------------------

    --------------------------------------------------

5.  Where in your garden or public spaces would you walk barefoot?

    --------------------------------------------------

    --------------------------------------------------

6.  List activities, other than gardening, that you would like to try in your garden (such as meditation or dancing).

    --------------------------------------------------

    --------------------------------------------------

# Room with a View

Transforming the immediate view from a laundry room with nature's help

## PROJECT DESCRIPTION

After my father had open-heart surgery, he spent a few days in the intensive care unit (ICU), and then was moved to a regular room for the rest of his recovery. ICUs are sterile areas with numerous specialized, technical, and monitoring equipment, with high traffic of doctors and nurses coming and going. It can be an intimidating and stressful environment for many patients and their loved ones. And, at least in the hospital my father was in, there were no windows to look outside for some distraction.

I remembered feeling scared, sad, and help-less, even though the outcome of the surgery was positive, the recovery process was going to be exhausting, both physically and mentally, for my father, and you never want to see a loved one going through tough times.

During visiting hours, aside from the physical and emotional support, I tried to put my psychology and horticultural therapy knowledge into good use to contribute to my father's recovery, doing what was in my power to uplift his spirit and mood while in the hos-pital. For example, I brought him an iPad with a long-format video of nature showing trees, birds singing, and water flowing, and garden books with big, colorful, dreamy photography. As I was trying to help my father relax, I was also distracting myself, focusing on the positive outcomes so far.

Starting with Roger Ulrich's 1984 journal article "View Through a Window May Influence Recovery from Surgery," which I read in my environmental psychology class in the mid-1990s, there are numerous research studies regarding the positive effects of views of nature (even through pictures, electronics, and virtual reality) on patients' recovery processes. Since then, I always pay close attention to the views from any room I step foot in.

I use the sink in my laundry room to clean small to medium-size garden containers and garden tools.

To summarize the article, after following the recovery process of patients after gall-bladder surgery, Ulrich's research found that patient rooms with access to a natural scene (trees) experienced lower levels of stress and pain, had a positive effect on mood, and those patients required fewer doses of pain medi-cation and were discharged a day earlier than those who had the same surgery but recovered in a room without a view of nature. You can imagine my reaction when I saw no windows in my father's ICU room.

The house sparrow (*Passer domesticus*) is a common bird spotted in suburban patios in Puerto Rico.

Ulrich also explained that these results can't be applied to all patient groups as equal and that not all natural scenes have the same desirable effect on people's moods, but he did recommend that "the quality of patient window views" should be taken into account. Since his breakthrough research, other similar studies have taken place and the accumulated evidence regarding the effect of nature on our physical, mental, and emotional health has not only helped reconfigure hospital design but also neighborhoods and workplace buildings.

Checking the quality of our window views at home is something we can do immediately and take the necessary steps to add or change what we can control. For instance, I decided to transform the view from my laundry room. This is a small area with a mid-wall glass window facing north.

I love the amount of bright indirect light that comes through the windows, especially during fall and winter. It's a great area to propagate plants. But as soon as you pull up the curtains, you see the fifteen-story apartment building across the street.

And because I want to keep my curtains up as much as possible, I added specific projects to my backyard garden, such as a flowering shrub, a birdbath (see "Backyard Birdbath," page 112), and a bird feeder, for constant and varied wildlife action, improving the quality of my views from the laundry room window almost immediately.

This makeover project has helped me refocus my attention on what is in my hands, literally, while making regular chores more enjoyable; it has helped me reduce my whining about things I can't control (the building); and when I'm hanging in this area I feel relaxed and happy.

## Your Window View

1. If the room you are in has a window, describe the view.

   ------------------------------------------

   ------------------------------------------

2. What is the main purpose of the room?

   ------------------------------------------

   ------------------------------------------

3. How much time do you spend in the room?

   ------------------------------------------

   ------------------------------------------

4. What do you like about the view you see? How would you enhance it?

   ------------------------------------------

   ------------------------------------------

5. What don't you like about the view? How much control do you have over that particular view?

   ------------------------------------------

   ------------------------------------------

6. List three things you can do immediately to change the quality of your view.

   ------------------------------------------

   ------------------------------------------

7. List the benefits of your new view.

   ------------------------------------------

   ------------------------------------------

## Things I Did to Enhance the View from the Laundry Room

1. In the garden, I installed a pink bougainvillea (*Bougainvillea* spp.) container shrub and let it grow over the garden wall.

2. I created a birdbath under the bougainvillea, repurposing an old tire (see "Backyard Birdbath," page 112), and a bird feeder, attracting a variety of urban birds with the bonus of a cheerful melody at all hours.

3. Planted containers with lantana (*Lantana*) and pennyroyal (*Mentha pulegium*) to create a green hedge—a pollinator magnet and a great show to watch from the laundry room window (see "Fragrant Garden Hedge," page 66).

4. Washed the laundry room windows, inside and out, letting in more bright light.

5. Adjusted the length of the curtains to frame a better view from the window.

6. Placed clear bottles filled with water around the space in which to propagate plants, and potted succulents and other cultivars into small terra-cotta containers to fill the inside windowsill.

7. Organized and cleaned surfaces that hold laundry products, more plants, and garden memorabilia.

# Fragrant Garden Hedge

## PROJECT DESCRIPTION

I have a container-grown hedge in my back-yard, to which I have dedicated time and effort to keep it practical and healthy. It serves as a divider, for privacy, and for camouflage, too. Yes, if I'm close to it, it helps dissipate any unpleasant scents coming from the neighbor-hood that I might not be able to control.

I created the green hedge using two main plants: a few varieties of lantana (*Lantana*), known in Puerto Rico and other parts of Latin America as *cariaquillo*, and pennyroyal (*Mentha pulegium*).

Both plants are sun-loving, with fragrant leaves and flowers, and are a sure magnet for pollinators such as bees and butterflies, providing a great treat to watch in spring and summer when both plants are covered with bright, colorful flowers.

I treat them as perennials, and in time, each plant develops a woody stem, which eventually creates a strong, supportive structure for other plants to tangle, fill, or rest on.

To promote leafiness, I trim the branches every now and then, and once a year I give it a heavy prune. It has been a delight to watch this hedge grow and form a bushy wall, making it a fun spectacle when birds and buzzing insects enjoy it, too.

When I'm seated by or passing along the hedge, I brush my palm over it, rubbing some of its leaves and flower petals between my fingers. The lantana blooms smell sweet and delicious, and that scent keeps butterflies coming back for more food.

This combination grows together beauti-fully and smells lovely. You can have the plants in the same container, just make sure it's big enough for both of them to have room to grow.

◁ Create a fragrant hedge in a container for your balcony or favorite garden spot.

At first sight, both plants may look similar, with oval dark green leaves, but as you look more closely, the lantanas are bigger, with round clusters of small, colored flowers.

I have each in its own planter. I wish I could surround the entire apartment building where I live with more hedges like this to shield my home from questionable smells that, some-times, breezy days carry in. Sometimes, I like to create a small bouquet to hang in my shower. Suddenly, the steam in the room turns aro-matic and very relaxing.

Having smelled and seen the potent effect of these two plants when entangled, I decided to replicate the combination in another, smaller, container by adding other fragrant plants to the mix.

If certain plants prove successful for you in all sorts of ways, like pleasantly scenting your spaces, keep experiencing them in different scenarios.

For this project, instead of using a big, round container, like the one in my backyard, I used the longest window box I could find and placed

*Mentha pulegium*, a mosquito-repelling plant, has lilac-blue flowers attached to its stem.

it securely over the railing on one side of my balcony.

The idea is to give a head-start for a fast-growing fragrant hedge. The container will be easy to remove, when needed, increase the privacy in the area, beautify the space, and might help reduce the mosquito victims at home. The other scented plants I added were common rue (*Ruta graveolens*) and lemon balm (*Melissa officinalis*).

When creating your window box, consider how the breeze flows into your home or patio area (or wherever you'll place it), because if you choose beautiful flowering plants but with an aroma you or someone in your family can't stand, it won't be a practical spot to spend time.

Research has shown that scent affects our well-being in general; they can help reduce blood pressure, ease stress and anxiety symptoms, as well as evoke happy memories. Choose your plants well and you will be able to use and enjoy your space frequently and with many benefits.

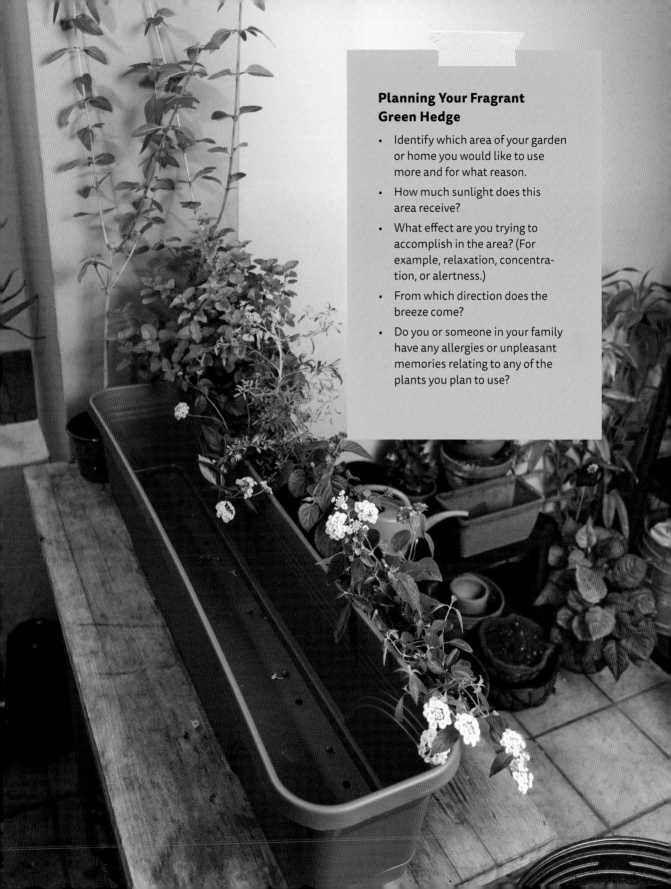

## Planning Your Fragrant Green Hedge

- Identify which area of your garden or home you would like to use more and for what reason.

- How much sunlight does this area receive?

- What effect are you trying to accomplish in the area? (For example, relaxation, concentration, or alertness.)

- From which direction does the breeze come?

- Do you or someone in your family have any allergies or unpleasant memories relating to any of the plants you plan to use?

## Other Plants You Can Use to Create a Mixed Fragrant Container Hedge

| PLANTS USED IN THE PROJECT | PURPOSE | ALTERNATIVES |
|---|---|---|
| Common rue, *Ruta graveolens* Lemon balm, *Melissa officinalis* | Contrast, edible herbs, filler, spiller | • Marjoram, *Origanum majorana* <br> • Oregano, *Origanum* <br> • Sweet pea, *Lathyrus odoratu* |
| Lantana, *Lantana* | Pop of color, filler | • Cottage pink, *Dianthus plumarius* <br> • Peony, *Paeonia* |
| Pennyroyal, *Mentha pulegium* | Woody stems develop over time to create a strong structure or frame | • Blue gum eucalyptus, *Eucalyptus globulus* <br> • Bay laurel, *Laurus nobilis* <br> • Lavender, *Lavandula* <br> • Rosemary, *Salvia rosmarinus* |

## Materials used in this project

- One 34-inch-long × 7-inch-wide × 6-inch-tall (86 × 18 × 15 cm) terra-cotta-colored plastic window box planter
- Potting soil
- Hand spade
- Two 5-inch (13 cm) pennyroyal (*Mentha pulegium*) plants
- Three 5-inch (13 cm) lantana (*Lantana*) plants
- One 5-inch (13 cm) lemon balm (*Melissa officinalis*) plant
- One 4-inch (10 cm) common rue (*Ruta graveolens*) plant
- Pine mulch (optional)

## Preparing the container

1. Fill the window box half to three-fourths full with potting soil.

2. Position the plants in the container the way you envision your design and check the correct planting depth for each plant.

3. Transplant your framing plants, the pennyroyal and lantana, first, then continue with the rest of the fragrant plants, making sure to cover their roots well with soil.

4. Remove the saucer from the container and water the plants until the soil drains. During warm periods, replace the saucer to retain humidity.

5. Mulch around the plants, if desired, to add a finishing touch and keep the soil from drying too fast.

6. Place the planter in a sunny area and, during your garden breaks, stop and smell the flowers. When placing the planter over a sill or railing, make sure to attach it securely to reduce accidents. If you live in an apartment building, check with the administration board for rules and installation suggestions.

# Barefoot Garden

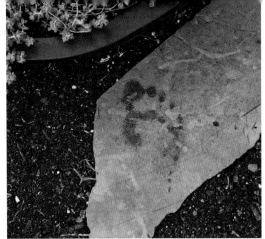

## PROJECT DESCRIPTION

My ideal garden floor is covered with grass, just like *doña* Lydia's. She lived across the street from my parents. As a kid, and when she wasn't home, I took off my shoes (if I was wearing them) and ran onto her pillowy grass. Sometimes, it felt fresh and smooth, not spiky, as other turf grasses can be. I stood there for as long as I could, in that well-manicured space, feeling the plants caressing my feet. That alone felt good and relaxing until the possibility of being caught stressed me out and I ran back home.

Until this day, I love to walk barefoot indoors and outdoors as much as I can, especially when watering my plants. Of course, to reduce potential injuries I make sure the surfaces aren't slippery, too hot, or contain any sharp objects that can harm me in any way.

If you have the space at home, this project is worth your time and money to transform an area just to be able to walk in shoeless. It's a great way to give relief to our feet after long hours wearing tight shoes, use muscles and bones that help us strengthen the whole body,

◁ I created a mobile thyme lawn in a container to step, rub, and relax my bare feet on. For this project, I repurposed a flat bonsai planter for a functional stress-relief patch, literally, at my feet.

### About Lemon Thyme

*Thymus citriodorus* is an herbaceous perennial with tiny fragrant variegated leaves. It thrives in sunny locations with well-drained soil, and can be grown as a culinary herb as well as a ground cover. It is a terrific addition to rock gardens and borders and can survive in temperatures as low as 20°F (-29°C).

and improve balance and circulation as well as body and space awareness. Going barefoot can even help us restore our proper gait.

But walking barefoot on natural surfaces has even further health benefits. *Earthing*, which is the concept of walking barefoot on grass, soil, or sand, is known to help reduce blood pressure, decrease stress and anxiety, and even pave the way to better sleep.

If you live in an apartment or a place with limited green areas, you can still have a small patch of green you can, literally, move around when needed. Instead of using grass for this gardening project, you can use an alternative

Trim the plant with garden shears to promote more vigorous leaf and stem growth and to keep the plant's growth habit compact.

You can also add flagstones as a stepping-stones for both feet, or balance on one foot while you rub the plants with the other. Before stepping onto the garden, and for the most enjoyment, consider your balance or mobility, in case you need assistance.

If you don't intend to step on the plants, beyond just a few strokes to caress your feet, use other plants (scented or unscented). Choose plants with a ground cover habit that suits your taste and grows well in the location where you'll keep the container most of the time.

This gardening project may require heavy lifting when it's completed and you want to move it, so I suggest placing it the area where you plan to use it. To ease its transport, use a plant caddy to move it around.

## DIY Plant Foot Massage

1. Place the garden container in the spot designated for your relaxing massage.

2. Place a comfortable chair near the container and take a seat.

3. Remove your shoes.

4. Place one or both feet on the stepping-stone.

5. Spray your feet with water.

6. Rub the soles of your feet against the plants.

7. Bend one leg and rest your foot on your opposite thigh. Massage your whole foot (toes, arch, and heel) with your hands or using a manual device for a few minutes. Repeat the process with the other foot.

8. Take your time to feel the plants against your bare feet, inhale the scent, if any, and relax.

plant material, such as the aromatic lemon thyme (*Thymus citriodorus*)—one of my favorite herbs to grow.

One advantage of using lemon thyme is that as you stroke it with your hand or the soles of your feet, it releases its scent, contributing to a more relaxing mood.

Of course, this container will need to be moved to a sunny area once you're done using it.

## Materials used for this project

- One 22-inch-long × 16-inch-wide × 4-inch-tall (56 × 40 × 10 cm) oval plastic bonsai pot
- Potting soil
- Hand spade
- One or two 11½ × 4½ × 2-inch (29 × 11 × 5 cm) irregular gray flagstones
- Eight to ten 5-inch (13 cm) lemon thyme (*T. citriodorus*) plants
- One 17-inch (43 cm) round plant caddy (optional)

## Preparing the container

1. Place the bonsai pot outdoors on the ground, or on a secure flat surface, in a sunny location.

2. Fill the container about three-fourths full with potting soil.

3. Position the flagstone(s) in the center of the container (see note).

4. Position the plants throughout the container, around the stepping-stone and near the borders.

5. Once your plants are in position, remove the flagstone and fill the space with more soil (see note).

6. Transplant the lemon thyme, covering the plants' roots with soil and leaving at least ½ inch (1 cm) of space between the soil and the container's rim.

7. Return the flagstone to the pot and water the plants. Let the soil drain well before moving the container indoors.

8. Use a plant caddy, if needed, to help move the container around. Do not step on the container while it is on the caddy.

**Note**: Remember, when you step on the stone, it will sink into the soil a little. You always want to keep the flagstone level with the soil, so you may need to add more soil occasionally.

# Sofrito Garden

## PROJECT DESCRIPTION

I may not eat or cook *arroz con habichuelas rojas* (rice and red beans) every day, but I can certainly recognize its smell anywhere, which comes from the combination of certain ingredients (some of them grown as far back as the Island's pre-Columbian era) used in its preparation, particularly in the way beans are cooked in Puerto Rico.

*Sofrito* is a culinary base used to flavor a variety of Puerto Rican dishes. It's most associated with the preparation of red beans, but you can use it in a variety of stews and other delicious recipes.

As soon as I start thinking about it, I begin to salivate. A recipe that is passed down through generations, making *sofrito* was learned orally or by imitation. It was formally introduced into Puerto Rican cookbooks in the 1930s. Before that, its preparation was taught in the kitchen as part of preparing a dish. Nowadays, you can buy it in the supermarket ready to use.

My parents prepare their version of *sofrito* using produce from their farm, to sell or give away. When I prepare *sofrito* from scratch, I don't follow a specific recipe, but use my instinct and memories—what I remember from my grandmother's kitchen or my parents' (they all love to cook).

According to Cruz Miguel Ortiz Cuadra, the late Puerto Rican gastronomic historian, the arrival of *sofrito* in our kitchens has elevated the flavors of our local food to the point of achieving global recognition.

The need to prepare and taste *sofrito* in our dishes becomes even more relevant when we are

◁ Deconstructing a traditional *sofrito* (a sauce of herbs, vegetables, fat, and seeds that provides distinctive flavor to Puerto Rican and other cuisines) to create a container garden was inspired by two of its main ingredients: *recao*, or culantro, and *ají dulce*, a type of sweet chile pepper.

### About *Sofrito*

*Sofrito* consists of culantro, or *recao* (*Eryngium foetidum*), peppers (*Capsicum chinense* and *Capsicum annuum*), achiote (*Bixa orellana*), tomatoes (*Lycopersicon esculentum*), capers, cilantro, cumin, garlic, oil, onions, and vinegar.

Source: C. Ortiz Cuadra, (2006)

away from home. I receive a lot of emails from Puerto Ricans living outside the Island (particularly in the United States) looking to grow culantro, or *recao*, one of *sofrito*'s key ingredients, in their gardens. Of course, they can buy bottled *sofrito* online, but there is just something special about growing at least one ingredient used in some of your ancestral dishes.

Growing plants that we recognize and associate with happy and tasty memories is a strategy we can incorporate into our life, especially to reduce stress and anxiety related

Culantro is a small herb that can grow in a depth of 1 foot (30 cm) or less, either in a sunny spot for abundant foliage, or one with filtered sunlight.

to cultural adjustments, starting in a new place, or nostalgia.

Creating a garden that reminds you of your country or your mother's cooking can comfort, and contributes to your social and emotional health.

When working with migrant populations, horticultural therapists, for example, create gardening opportunities to support individuals through their process of acculturation. Mostly as part of vocational programs, the gardening projects provide participants the opportunity to learn new skills that can be transferred into horticulture-related jobs, practice a new language, and develop new social connections.

According to research, participating in this kind of program strengthens one's self-confidence, provides a sense of purpose, and helps develop a faster sense of belonging in a new country or place.

My *sofrito* garden can be your inspiration for any comfort recipe garden—one that can transport you to your family's recipes

or a particular childhood memory. For me, knowing the history of *sofrito* strengthens my identity and senses. It also gives me the opportunity to share relevant information in a creative way, making me even more proud of where I come from.

For this gardening project, I combined two principal ingredients in one container: the sweet pepper (*ají dulce*) and culantro (*recao*). Because the pepper is a medium-size plant, it needs enough space for its roots to grow and develop.

I used a medium-size terra-cotta planter and planted the pepper plant in the center, then added a few culantro plants around it.

Both plants need humidity, and organic matter in the soil—a perfect combination to maximize the growing space.

In a garden bed, you can try to incorporate more of the basic *sofrito* ingredients, but even growing only one is worth the time and effort. It will definitely add more flavor to your life.

For this project, I experimented successfully with the *olla* irrigation technique, using a no-drainage terra-cotta container filled with water and buried into the soil. This way, the plants absorb the water they need without me worrying about it. The dent in the container's lid can also serve as a small bird feeder.

## Materials used for this project

- One 8 × 12-inch (20 × 30 cm) round terra-cotta pot
- Potting soil
- Hand spade
- One 5-inch (13 cm) *ají dulce* (*Capsicum chinense*) plant
- Two or three 5-inch (13 cm) culantro (*Eryngium foetidum*) plants
- One 4-inch-diameter × 4¼-inch-high (10 × 10.8 cm) terra-cotta vase without drainage holes
- 1 small terra-cotta saucer (to use as a lid)
- Stool (optional)

## Preparing the container

1. Place the round terra-cotta pot on a secure, flat surface, and fill it three-fourths full with potting soil.

2. Place the *ají* plant in the center of the container and the culantro plants around it, near the pot's edge.

3. Insert the terra-cotta vase into the soil between the *ají* and one of the culantro plants, leaving 1½ inches (3.5 cm) of the vase extending above the soil. Fill the vase with water and place the saucer (lid) on top. (You can use the lid as a bird feeder, too).

4. Cover all the plants' roots with soil, leaving at least ½ inch (1 cm) of space between the soil and the container's rim.

5. Water the container and place it in a sunny location where it will receive 6 to 8 hours of sunlight each day.

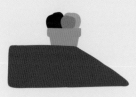

# Meditation Garden

## PROJECT DESCRIPTION

Walking shoeless in my garden is my most frequent meditation style. These sorts of garden breaks can take me from 5 to 30 minutes, so I tend to have as many micro doses each day as possible. I'm fortunate to have a small garden that I can cross in a couple of minutes, with abundant nature-based opportunities for a lifetime, and I plan to use it even more for meditation and other well-being practices.

Meditation is a centuries-old practice used for calming the mind and enhancing awareness of ourselves and our physical surroundings. Sometimes, the term is used interchangeably with "mindfulness," but meditation is a practice under the broad concept of being present in the moment (a.k.a. mindfulness).

According to scientific evidence, meditation can help reduce anxiety and depression and increase pain tolerance. It can also lower blood pressure, increase creativity and imagination, and improve sleep.

There are different types of meditation—from being mindful of our breath to compassion-focused to body scanning to mantra chanting and, of course, there's walking meditation, which consists of taking off your shoes and walking barefoot, feeling and paying attention to the ground and how we react to it.

In slowing my pace, as I walk, I become aware of my green space, from under my feet to what is ahead of me. Suddenly, I become focused on specific plants, bird songs, and insects buzzing. Within minutes, I start feeling the positive effects nature has on me: from freshness to peace, calm, and awe, to enlightened and feeling energized. The more I use the garden as a tool for my well-being (besides gardening), such as for contemplation or meditation, the more ease I have in managing things I can't control.

Meditation and mindfulness expert Caragh Behan states, "Over time, the regular practice of meditation allows individuals to react to their environment and anything that arises in the course of their day with more calm and equanimity."

With practice, you can disconnect your mind anywhere, but having a place in contact with nature, where you can go and sit to calm down, physically and mentally, can bring even more benefits.

Philosopher Byung-Chul Han wrote, "in the garden, I rest from the tires of life," a reflection on his gardening experience compiled in his book *Loa a la tierra*. It's incredible how the same place that can tire me after a grueling session of gardening can also be the restorative place where I leave behind all my mental fatigue.

The practice of meditation is a low-cost activity that can be adapted to anyone (adult, child, teen, people with special needs) to support their wellness plan, and certainly, you can transform any space, even a dead-end alley, a balcony, or indoor nook, to create your own breathing room.

There are some key elements to consider when creating a meditation garden, but most important, this particular garden room should appeal to you. From the space and plants to any features that will help you disconnect and reconnect with yourself.

My husband, Antonio, who practices meditation twice a day, shared with me what he considered the most important characteristics of a meditation space: comfort, tranquility, protection, and consistency.

Meditation gardens vary from one place to another, but most of the literature regarding how to create one agrees that the space should offer a least a few of the following features:

◁ Transforming a dead-end garden alley into a calming meditation space

I created my meditation garden at the end of a long alley with no exit. A tall white fence gives the space the seclusion it needs from the view of the parking lot

- A sense of enclosure, or privacy
- A cool temperature, with a breeze
- A focal point
- A clean, clutter-free environment
- A chair or a comfortable area to rest
- A water feature (birdbath or fountain)
- Plants and trees that promote calmness (the colors blue, pink, and green are associated with calm and freshness)

Remember, you're creating a personal space. Make adjustments based on your life circumstances, available space, budget, and the best plant specimens suited for your region and microclimate.

Because I live on the first floor of a walk-up apartment building, I moved and rearranged a variety of tall grasses and small bushes that, eventually, will add more privacy to the area. I already had most of these plants in several parts of my garden, such as the fountain grass (*Pennisetum setaceum*), which adds movement and a sense of flow as the wind blows, saving me time and money while using the space better.

To transform my small lot, I prepared the garden floor, in the alley, using gravel with the double purpose of ornamentation and maintenance; the mulching keeps the weeds to the minimum.

To be able to sit or stretch, I found a wooden pallet in great condition that fit the space perfectly. As for the bushes and other types of vegetation, I didn't go far for inspiration. I had a great experience with copperleaf (*Acalypha wilkesiana*) in my front yard, so I knew this plant would work for the meditation room. It grows fast and tends to be bushy if well trimmed. I planted two, each in a 15-gallon (57 L) container, where they will eventually grow and cover part of the fence, providing some shade and privacy.

To add a water feature, instead of a fountain, I moved three self-watering containers to the area and replanted them with a fragrant herbs, fruits, and vegetables. Other pre-potted plants were also added.

Remember, the more you use the space, the more aware you will be of it, which will help you edit what it contains, depending on what speaks to you at a particular moment.

Now, with everything in place in this part of the garden, I decided to focus my meditation time on growth.

## Materials used for this transformational project

- Landscape fabric (optional)
- Fine gravel; ¼-inch (6 mm) or smaller
- Pine bark mulch
- Four 3-gallon (11 L) copperleaf (*Acalypha wilkesiana*) plants
- Five 3-gallon (11 L) fountain grass (*Pennisetum setaceum*) plants
- 9 different 5-inch (13 cm) herbs and fruits
- Two 15-gallon (57 L) propagation containers
- 4 potted plants, perhaps relocated from another area of the patio
- Potting soil and garden soil
- Hand spade
- 1 repurposed wooden pallet
- 1 yoga mat (optional)

## Preparing the area and containers

1. Clean the area where you'll plant your meditation garden: remove grass, rocks, weeds, and any other objects you won't need in the space.

2. Prepare the garden floor: Place a permeable liner in the area to reduce weed growth, or cover the areas with mulch, such as gravel or pine bark.

3. Transplant, re-pot, and groom any vegetative material you're bringing into the area. This includes preparing the self-watering containers or any other water feature.

4. Move and relocate potted plants from other parts of your house and do some grooming, if necessary.

5. Water all the plants.

6. Add any permanent or semi-permanent furniture or accessories to make your space comfortable and ready to meditate in.

# Serve the Community

During the past few years, most of my volunteer time has been spent within organizations or communities related to education, the environment, or gardening.

THAT SERVICE HAS taken many forms, from following the lead and organizing events to evaluating proposals or giving advice. Service was part of my upbringing.

I remember my parents volunteering constantly for many of the activities my brothers and I were involved in—whether at school or in our community. My father would serve as a baseball or volleyball coach for our neighborhood team, including being the driver for many of our teammates, along with my mother, if a second car was needed, and she always stepped up for everything school-related. Besides their kids' interests, my parents also volunteered at work, church, or when friends and family needed an extra hand, and they still help out where they can.

Volunteering, in school, college, and work, as well as in the many communities I have been part of, has helped me communicate and socialize with people from different backgrounds, of different ages and interests, and make new friends and feel more satisfied with who I am as an individual.

Another great benefit of volunteering (in any life circumstance) includes building self-confidence and gaining valuable job skills that can help advance your career or inform what you're really passionate about.

When you serve the community of your interest, you're more invested, creative, and socially connected and, according to research, have a higher probability of living a happier, longer life than those who don't. Also, it's not surprising, the more comfortable we feel as part of a community, the more generous we are to it—whether with more time for serving, money, or both.

Gardening projects are a great vehicle to fulfill and combine our interests in doing more community service while increasing our connection with nature. As a volunteer, you can help keep up a community park, transform a vacant plot into a community garden, plant sit for someone who's ill, or teach adults who have disabilities to propagate, water, and cultivate plants in a greenhouse. The projects are endless, and our communities need us.

The next few projects can and should be adjusted to your community's needs—from creating a container garden to transform the façade of an organization you care for to creating space for your colleagues to relax before heading to the budget meeting to putting together a garden kit to bring others calm and joy during a stressful situation.

I always recommend that you ask several members within your group about their thoughts before investing in resources. Your community can be the local businesses in your neighborhood, your congregation, the garden club, or some colleagues at work.

Even if everybody within is excited about one or all of these ideas, certain projects could need formal permits to proceed. Just make sure to inform yourself to serve and grow your community better. **v**

## Self-Assessment Time

Do a self-assessment to learn how you can be more involved within your community by answering these questions.

1. What type of work would you do without being asked?

   ---------------------------------------------

   ---------------------------------------------

2. Describe your most recent volunteering experience.

   ---------------------------------------------

   ---------------------------------------------

3. List places or organizations within your community where you would like to volunteer.

   ---------------------------------------------

   ---------------------------------------------

4. What demographic would you be most interested to volunteer with? (Kids, older adults, local entrepreneurs.)

   ---------------------------------------------

   ---------------------------------------------

5. What gardening activity, that you enjoy, would you share when volunteering?

   ---------------------------------------------

   ---------------------------------------------

6. What gardening tasks would you be willing to help with?

   ---------------------------------------------

   ---------------------------------------------

# Life Happens

## PROJECT DESCRIPTION

When I started to write formally about gardening, I was in my mid-thirties, and had visited this amazing community garden in Puerto Rico, on the premises of an apartment building where hundreds of families lived. The garden was a result of the coordinated effort of a small group of residents. I was in awe of the beautiful plants they grew, the strategic companion planting they applied, and how they repurposed whatever they could—from old refrigerators to tires and paint buckets. We toured around and checked on what was growing on the propagation tables, while pollinators minded their business.

During the guided tour, one of the community leaders explained to the media guests how the garden served their immediate community, a great number of older adults with some younger families mixed in. Residents who volunteered to work in the garden could

◁ Start listing and adjusting your favorite gardening tasks and activities as your life circumstances change without losing your joy.

harvest for free and the rest of the residents would have priority to buy some of the harvest before any nonresidents. That visit was a turning point for me on thinking about how I wanted, and needed, to grow my own garden, and a better way to explain to my readers what this kind of endeavor entailed.

The community leader shared, too, some of the daily struggles they faced regarding certain gardening tasks and how other regular maintenance responsibilities were falling behind because they lacked the right help. Because most of the garden volunteers were older, or were experiencing a variety of health and mobility issues, and not many of the younger residents were interested or able to participate, the garden was becoming a burden to keep in shape. And even though some tasks became burdens to be shed for some, the joy of participating in many of the other activities that can take place in a community garden became equally important.

Nowadays, as I walk around my own garden, I'm amazed at all the lessons and experiences learned since visiting that community garden. I think about all the small and big changes

◁ When weeding or doing other garden activities close to the ground, use a kneeling pad to protect your knees and reduce excessive bending. Try to change your position and stretch every 20 minutes.

achieved over time, consciously and unconsciously, just to be able to enjoy more and hurt less when gardening. Yes, one day you wake up ready to take on anything in the garden—from trimming bushes with worn-down shears to carrying a few 30-pound (14 kg) bags of soil on your shoulders to weeding for hours kneeling on the ground—until you can't anymore, without needing at least a week of rest and some muscle relaxer, to recuperate.

As we grow older or health circumstances push us to adjust our daily routine to be able to continue functioning physically, mentally, and emotionally, there are certain changes that can take us more time to accept. Sometimes, we come quickly to our senses; other time it takes a minor accident to make us face reality.

In the last few years, I have started to face that reality, particularly when it comes to gardening. I have to be more careful about how and where I walk when watching my dog going around the garden, keep trees and bushes to a certain height so I'm able to trim them safely without the need to step on a ladder, and, most definitely, using a kneeling pad while weeding.

Because I want to keep gardening, I'm happy to make the necessary adjustments to stay on that path, instead of throwing in the towel and quitting a hobby that brings me so much joy and well-being.

Changes in our gardening lifestyle don't need to be drastic, if there is no need, but we do have to be aware of how decisions made today, regarding the purchase of a tool, the addition of certain plants, or the choosing of hardscapes, will affect our quality of life in a long term.

Although this is an individual process, which I recommend doing thoroughly and as often as possible by yourself or with professional help, there are general areas where we all can start to make small adjustments as our life unfolds in the garden. Remember that the more comfortable we are doing what we like, the more time we will spend on it and with greater satisfaction, regardless of what life brings.

1. **Paths:** Consider leveling and paving the area where you walk daily to get to garden beds, ponds, or rooms around the garden. Reduce the potential to trip or fall on bumps or slippery zones.

2. **Branch down:** Reduce the height of trees and shrubs to make them easier to trim or harvest without ladders. Remove branches or plants that interfere with visibility when passing from one area to another.

3. **Transportation:** Use a small wheelbarrow to transport heavy materials, such as bags of soil, potted plants, or things for disposal.

4. **Gardening tools and accessories:** Switch to ergonomic and colorful tools as you replace those you already have. Add reels for hose storage and install smart water systems or accessories instead of carrying heavy watering cans around.

5. **Comfortable seating:** Add more seating areas in which to rest and that provide comfortable respite as you go through your garden activities.

Use this chart to write down at least five garden activities or tasks that you enjoy most in your garden; indicate those you will need to adjust over time and how you will do that; and designate which you will need to delegate to someone else because of your current circumstances.

| Garden Task/ Activity | When do I enjoy it? | Required Adjustments | Need to be Delegated |
|---|---|---|---|
| Weeding | In the morning | Kneeling pad and stretch every 20 minutes | Summer season |
| | | | |
| | | | |
| | | | |
| | | | |
| | | | |
| | | | |
| | | | |
| | | | |

# Garden Lift

The mandevilla (*Mandevilla*) is a beautiful flowering plant that can climb around the post.

## PROJECT DESCRIPTION

We all know a small business or a whole community business strip near our neighborhood that offers amazing services and products, but with a front entrance or façade in desperate need of a makeover that may even help drive more patronage.

Bringing people to your doorstep can be seen as winning half the battle. Many business owners understand that, for customers, the outer appearance of the store is as important as the inside and so they do everything they can to budget or gather the help of friends and family to keep their business looking fresh and inviting.

Structural renovations, especially if you don't own the building, or even a fresh coat of paint every year, can be expensive. However, planting trees and adding a few gardening projects can be a more affordable way to achieve the look you want.

According to the report "The Economics of Biophilia" published by Terrapin, a sustainability consulting firm in the United States, consumer studies regarding biophilic design found that customers find stores and streets that add green features (trees and potted plants) to their shopping experiences to be friendlier, safe, and worthy of their money.

Other results shared in the report mention that consumers will stay longer, shop more often, and even pay more for the goods from businesses that use nature as part of their design. "The addition of plant life into the realm of retail shopping appears to act as a stimulus that boosts the image perception and economic viability of stores." Well-cared-for plants inside or outside the business send a message to the potential customers on how they will be treated once in the store.

Check social media platforms, like Instagram, and you will see thousands of photos from people sharing incredible pictures of building façades or the interior of a store where natural elements are part of their shopping experience.

Other than retail stores, different types of businesses, as well as community organizations that run a brick-and-mortar operation, can benefit from biophilic design strategies, too, without depleting their operational budgets.

This next gardening project can serve as an inspiration for a quick and affordable façade transformation. The number and variety of

Spiller plants, such as the sedum (*Sedum rupestre*) and creeping Jenny (*Lysimachia nummularia*), which don't need too much depth, are tucked around the container to cover any exposed soil and create a sensation of abundance.

plants used can be adjusted based on the container use and the end location (sunny or shady). The main purpose of the project is to draw attention to and complement the intended customer experience and not interfere with it.

I reused a glazed clay planter with drainage for arranging a group of appealing, colorful, textured plants for a sunny location. Although, I must admit my horticultural transgression of planting five plants in a 14-inch (35 cm) planter. But hear me out, this is meant to be a showstopper, with the purpose of grabbing attention now, and then in a few months, changing some or all of the plants to keep it fresh for the eyes of the customers.

Eventually, each plant used in this project can be transplanted to create other arrangements.

Besides the plants, the second most important element of this project is the addition of the signpost inserted into the soil. This is a great opportunity to be creative and inventive when trying to capture people's attention.

I purchased the post and, luckily, found a wooden panel in a secondhand store that fit perfectly as the sign. I added the small ceramic pot because it can draw curiosity, but a well-designed logo would do the same. Around the logo or pot, a welcome message and/or the business hours will help to serve your customers better.

For the planter arrangement, I used plants to grab attention from a distance and ignite curiosity once you're close. Some are taller and add movement to the scene, such as the dwarf papyrus and the fountain grasses—their growth acts as thrillers and fillers.

Heavy arrangements like this are recommended to be secured and placed on a planter caddy to facilitate moving it around the business premises.

Whether for your business or an organization you're volunteering for, everyone can use a garden lift from time to time.

## Materials used in this project

- Drop cloths
- One 12 × 12-inch (30 × 30 cm) wooden sign panel
- Off-white latex outdoor paint
- Paintbrush
- One 14-inch (35 cm) burgundy glazed clay planter
- Potting soil
- Hand spade
- One 1-gallon (3.8 L) fountain grass (*Pennisetum setaceum*) plant
- One 1-gallon (3.8 L) dwarf papyrus (*Cyperus isocladus*) plant
- One 6-inch (15 cm) pink mandevilla (*Mandevilla*) plant
- One 4-foot (120 cm) signpost with hanger
- One 5-inch (13 cm) burgundy creeping Jenny (*Lysimachia nummularia*) plant
- One 5-inch (13 cm) lemon ball sedum (*Sedum rupestre*) plant
- Rolling plant caddy (optional)
- Markers or paints in various colors, to paint a design or message on the sign
- Small paintbrushes
- Small blue glazed flat-back pot, approximately 4 inches long × 3½ inches wide (10 × 8.9 cm) (optional)

## Preparing the container

1. Cover the area where you'll be painting with drop cloths.

2. Paint the wooden sign panel and let it dry completely.

3. Clean and disinfect the 14-inch (35 cm) clay planter and let dry.

4. Fill the clean planter half full with potting soil and transplant the fountain grass into it, close to the edge, then cover its roots with more soil.

5. Transplant the dwarf papyrus into the planter, across from the fountain grass, also near the edge of the planter, then cover its roots with soil.

6. At one side of the planter, transplant the mandevilla, then cover its roots with soil. At this point, you should have a cluster of plants in the planter.

7. Insert the signpost in the center of the planter, between the fountain grass and the papyrus plant. Try to catch part of the root balls to help stabilize the post. Train the longest stems of the mandevilla around the post to use as a trellis.

8. Tuck the creeping Jenny and sedum plants around the planter to fill the bare spots, and cover the roots with soil as you go.

9. Place the container on the planter caddy (if using) and secure it. Water the plants heavily until the soil drains.

10. Label the wooden sign, or paint a welcome message or the business's name on it. Let dry, then add the sign panel to the post. For my sign panel, I attached a small glazed ceramic pot right at its center with a chunk of sedum in it, secured with a nail. There is still space for painting or labeling a short message around the little planter.

# Healing Nook

## PROJECT DESCRIPTION

Homes, businesses, schools, and all sorts of institutions have one, or too many, misused, or unused, outdoor corners. Corners are typically used for placing anything that will need storage. In other cases, the corner is left empty until a creative idea to fill it kicks in, and who knows when that will be?

Creating a healing garden in a corner space is a practical solution. Anyone can benefit from the exposure to nature, no matter the size of the garden, but the green space will make a positive difference.

Research shows that things such as easy access to the space, water features, vegetation, and significant biodiversity have a positive effect on people's perception and satisfaction with the area, characteristics that increase its use and share its benefits with more people.

◁ Transform an empty corner into a healing garden space.

Myriad studies show that being in contact with nature experiences, even for five minutes a day, can help us relax, heal physically and mentally, restore our spirit, enhance self-esteem, and lead to living longer, more fulfilling lives.

Well-planned and intended healing gardens take into consideration the needs of their participants as well as the location and environmental conditions to maximize the space and resources.

The therapeutic effects of a healing garden are different for each person, but the purpose is the same: to improve total well-being.

If the healing corners are located in a workplace, some employees might use them to increase their daily doses of sunlight and fresh air, ease stress, or to take a mental break after a long meeting. In a hospital or treatment facility, patients can use the space to aid their recovery process, deal in private with a diagnosis, or contemplate a natural scene that will help enhance positive emotions.

When in doubt about what to do with a blank corner, plant a garden.

For this project, I saved an outdoor corner at my house and transformed it into a useful green space. Before that, however, I used it to pile up unused containers or lean big gardening tools against the wall—never a long-term solution. But as I've added more sitting areas to my garden to enjoy the view from several angles, the view over that corner wasn't flattering at all.

My vision for the space was simple and clear: I wanted to place a small bench against the wall to enhance feelings of privacy and comfort. Next to it, I wanted a garden bed with flowering, textured, colorful plants to enjoy and be able to touch from my seat.

This particular nook receives sunlight in the morning and, as the day progresses, becomes shaded and cool. Also, it's windy. Environmental factors need to be considered when choosing your plant material.

This healing corner at home can be a starting point for other locations. You can leave the seat permanently or remove it, as needed.

## Considerations for Creating a Healing Nook

1. Describe who will use this green space and their needs.

2. Evaluate the corner conditions (amount of light, soil structure [if outdoors], immediate views, potential hazards, space measurements, other).

3. Consider traffic, accessibility, and water availability vs. needs for the garden.

4. Inventory existing vegetation or structures. Are all useful or do some need to be removed? Is anything necessary missing?

5. Detail plans for building and maintaining the space, including volunteers and budget.

## Materials used in this project

- Plastic border, to define the garden bed (optional)
- Garden soil
- Hand spade
- One 15-gallon (57 L) Panama rose (*Rondeletia strigosa*) plant
- One 5-inch (13 cm) Lemon Ball sedum (*Sedum rupestre* 'Lemon Ball') plant
- Four 1 gallon-size (3.78 L) ornamental grasses (*Pennisetum* spp.)
- Four 5-inch (5.7 cm) pots of coleus (*Coleus*) varieties
- Five 5-inch (5.7 cm) pots of firecracker (*Cuphea*) plants
- Fine gravel; ¼-inch (6 mm) or less
- Bench or chair
- Bench or chair cushion (optional)

## Preparing the area

1. Clean up the area, removing any weeds, rocks, or other debris.
2. Level the terrain.
3. Mark the garden area and place the border around it (if using).
4. Add garden soil or compost to the area.
5. Position the plants and transplant them into the garden. Place the potted Panama Rose at the center of the garden bed and use the sedum as a ground cover around the inside of the planter. Then, position the other ground cover plants, starting with the tallest ones (*Pennisetum*), then the coleus. Finish it up with the smallest ones (firecrackers).
6. Add more soil, as needed.
7. Add gravel where you plan to place a chair and level the gravel.
8. Water the garden to help establish the plants.
9. Add the seat and any other accessories you like to make the space comfortable and inviting.

# Garden Break Room

## PROJECT DESCRIPTION

A couple of months into the pandemic, I binge-watched the entire *Grey's Anatomy* series on Netflix. Along the way, I learned medical jargon as I cried my eyes out. During those long hours escaping the moment's reality, I was still reminded of the social, political, and health issues taking place around the time each episode was originally scheduled to air on television. Writers wrote facts that made you think, even if you didn't want to.

As a person who promotes plants and gardening for well-being, I was happy to see how using plants for wellness was written into one of the episodes (season 15, episode 18). The plant room episode was contextualized for the hospital environment including how patients, as well as doctors and nurses, could benefit from plant life at the health care facility.

I knew that the script was based on published reports of studies regarding how the presence or view of plants pre- and post-operation can improve a patient's physical well-being, decrease anxiety, lower blood pressure, and even help them manage pain.

The made-for-television plant room was also shown to be useful to the doctors as a break room and, of course, added a green layer when discussing their personal drama out of the OR.

It doesn't come as a surprise that health care workers today are more likely to experience mental health problems linked directly to their work conditions. According to the Centers for Disease Control and Prevention (CDC) in the United States, workers such as doctors and nurses are caught up in "constant stressful and emotional situations regarding patients' treatment, high-risk exposure to infectious diseases, demanding physical work, long and unpredictable work hours and, for some, financial

◁ Create an alluring area in your workplace for people to pause and slow down.

When creating the space, personalize it and make any necessary adjustments when thinking about the public, location (outdoors or indoors), and budget.

strains" that can also increase other personal stresses. These professionals are prone to experience burnout syndrome (chronic stress in the workplace not managed appropriately) due to excess workload, lack of control, and not enough employer support—conditions that apply also to many workers, especially during the pandemic.

As the scientific evidence regarding the benefits of nature to well-being keeps growing, fortunately, the applied and practical strategies for using it do, too. In the middle of the world health emergency, many of us used nature activities, like gardening, to cope with the stress in our lives, and continue doing it even now as a daily wellness strategy.

One of the many solutions I apply, and recommend to participants in my workshops, is to take garden breaks (in your backyard, a park, or forest) as much as possible because it's proven that spending at least five minutes on nature-based activities can reduce irritation and improve attention, concentration, and productivity.

But to promote and facilitate the garden breaks, anywhere, it's important to create the

A lush mint container placed near the seating area will provide a sensorial experience. Add a fun element, like this little gnome, to spark curiosity and some laughter.

Accessories like a straw fence will not only help you with privacy, but also add a natural look to the area. Secure it to a permanent structure at the top, center, and bottom with wires, cable ties, or jute.

environment for them, as happened in the *Grey's Anatomy* episode. You either bring the plants in or look outdoors for that purpose.

To help you start and define a garden break room, use the following checklist to cover the basic needs to create a space that you, and the people in your life, whether family members or colleagues, feel attracted to and that makes you stop whatever you're doing and pause, consciously, to relax for five to twenty minutes, a few days each week.

▷ Surround the space with small potted trees and bushes. Here a potted pomegranate tree (*Punica granatum*) will add another layer of privacy and natural enhancement to the space, and eventually will produce an easy-picking snack.

## Checklist: Garden Break Room

1. **Location and lighting:** Select a visible area that ignites curiosity from different vantage points, one that's not as busy as other areas and with easy access for everybody, regardless of physical capability. If the space is outdoors and meant to be used after dark, install proper lighting as a security measure.

2. **Paths and flooring:** Facilitate the use of the break room with an accessible route. Keep paths cleared, weeded, and, if necessary, paved and/or mulched.

3. **Seating:** Add comfortable seats with cushions, like lounge chairs, so people can stretch their legs into a semi-horizontal position, if they want to. Set up the space so more than one person is able to use it at once.

4. **Fencing:** Define the garden break room with low fences, potted plants, or with small shrubs. If any side of the room is exposed to a parking lot or ugly wall, camouflage that view and provide a sense of privacy to the area using a decorative reed or bamboo fence.

5. **Shade:** If there are no big trees in the area to provide cooling shade, install pergolas, umbrellas, or sails to encourage people to get outside on a sunny day and stay for more than five minutes, if they can.

6. **Plants and shrubs:** Close to the seating areas, add small potted plants, such as aromatic and edible herbs, and small fruit trees, too, that contribute to stimulating the senses and that can even be harvested for use in iced drinks.

7. **Fun elements:** Try to make people laugh, even if they are alone. It's good for their mental health and their facial muscles. Include visible or hidden figures, like gnomes, in the pots or scattered around the area. Even the smallest detail can help people disconnect from work temporarily, or any other cause of stress, bringing focus to things other than themselves.

8. **Entertainment:** Promote reading actual books instead of using electronics while in the room by providing books or magazines on non-work-related subjects. Start a library exchange program. (For ideas, see "Little Library Garden," page 46.)

9. **Wildlife features:** Install water features, such as a fountain, to camouflage noises. Add a birdbath and a bird feeder to attract wildlife to the area, like urban birds and other pollinators (for more ideas, see "Backyard Birdbath," page 112).

10. **Healthy snacking:** Include potted garden fruits and vegetables for easy picking and snacking (blueberries, cherry tomatoes). Until harvesting time, leave water and other healthy snacks in visible, but guarded, places. Provide disposal alternatives in the area, too.

Use a post to hang a basket for water and other snacks. Here, a wire basket is used to hold a metal bowl filled with goodies.

# Garden-tainment Box

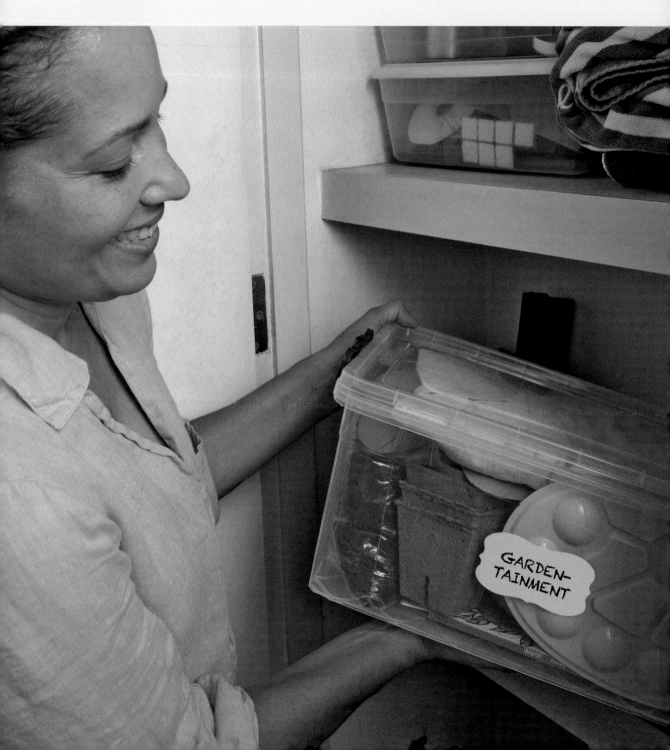

## PROJECT DESCRIPTION

A well-planned activity can transform your mood and enhance sensory, motor, cognitive, and social skills, plus, depending on the purpose of the exercise, it can be an effective strategy to improve concentration.

Regardless of the purpose, there are so many activities to choose from that, sometimes, we end up spending more time choosing which will be the best to suit a particular situation than we spend doing the activity. We need entertainment in our lives because it helps restore our mind, body, and spirit.

According to American psychologist Abraham Maslow's hierarchy of needs, having sufficient rest time is part of our basic physiological needs, which are depicted at the base of the pyramid, as they're foundational and must be attended to before needs higher up can be met.

Activity boxes, for example, have proven over the years to be a popular and practical solution for entertainment, and if they include other components that reinforce learning, creativity, and imagination skills, demand can be higher.

Entertainment in a box is not only a great solution for parents who are looking to reduce screen time for their kids, but for adults, too. If we're trying to engage kids through activities that will encourage brain development and teach them how to relate to others, these same activities can definitively help grown-ups in areas such as reducing brain degeneration and maintaining active social interactions.

Activity boxes can be lifesavers in everyday situations, too, such as traveling with kids, or during a power outage, or to help energize a

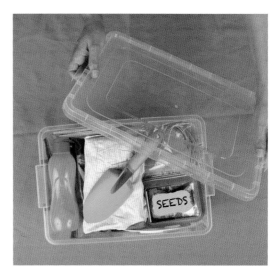

When preparing your kit, choose a box or other container with a lid, big enough to store all the supplies for the activities and that is waterproof.

gathering that is losing steam. They can be helpful in hospitals for patients as well as caregivers, in child and adult care centers, and shelters. Also, relief teams can use activity boxes as tools to help people manage the stress and anxiety that occurs during and after an emergency, whether natural or human-made.

Whatever the reasons, the success of an activity box depends closely on what you know about the audience it is intended for. This will help define its purpose, identify the theme and materials, and reveal any adjustments needed based on skill level.

The decision on whether to buy a pre-made activity box or build your own is personal and may depend on the intended audience, the number of kits needed, the frequency of purchase, budget, knowledge regarding the content, and time available to complete the activities.

For this activity box project, and for obvious reasons, I chose the theme and purpose of gardening and crafting activities in case of an emergency. (Note: It is up to you, or the organization you work for, to define what constitutes

◁ Put together an activity box filled with a variety of garden and crafting supplies to entertain family, friends, or members of your community.

Fill the box with lightweight supplies for easy transport and store it in an accessible place. Do not include tools, accessories, or any supplies you use on a daily basis. Include new or duplicates instead.

Remember to identify the activity box with a label, especially if storing it with other boxes and products.

## Designing Your Activity Box

1. Choose a theme or subject.
2. Define the age group for the activities and the desired outcomes.
3. Specify activities, skill levels, and basic instructions.
4. Detail your budget for supplies, tools, and accessories.
5. Choose safe and nontoxic supplies.

an emergency based on established priorities.) This means the supplies stored in the box will be used during the special circumstance you designate.

The contents of the box I prepared include supplies that can be used to design activities that children and adults can enjoy together or separately. From active to passive, with low to moderate physical impact, and for various skill levels.

If you feel inspired to prepare a similar box, consider which kind of garden and crafting activities and supplies will be appropriate to the circumstances, the safety of the materials, and how many supplies will be needed based on the potential number of people, and the potential number of days, this garden-*tainment* kit may be needed.

## Materials used in this project

- A few small plastic containers with lids
- Acrylic paint in primary colors
- Paintbrushes
- Small sponges
- Chalk
- Colored pencils
- A variety of seed packets
- Washable glue sticks
- Wooden craft sticks
- Colorful decorations
- Removable adhesive labels (for labeling the box and its contents)
- Clear plastic container box, 16 × 11 × 6½ inches (40 × 28 × 16 cm), with lid
- Paper bags
- Blank cards
- Coloring books
- Small biodegradable bag
- Potting soil in a plastic bag
- Container for water
- A number of 3 × 3-inch (7.5 × 7.5 cm) terra-cotta and biodegradable containers
- Trowel
- Spoon
- Ruler
- Tape
- Scissors
- Tweezers
- Hand duster
- Cotton apron
- Small towel

## Preparing the kit

When organizing the contents, keep key supplies visible so you have an immediate idea of the variety and potential activities available before opening the box.

1. Distribute and organize the smaller supplies in the small containers. You can group them by category, type of activity, or function, for example: painting materials (acrylic paints, brushes, and sponges) or crafting accessories (glue stick, wooden craft sticks, colorful decorations). Label the containers.

2. Once the contents are grouped and labeled, organize them and any bigger items in the bigger container box. First, place all the flat supplies, such as the coloring book, paper bags, blank cards, apron, and others, in the box.

3. Add the big and bulky supplies (nonfragile), such as the potting soil bag (make sure to seal it first), the water container, and the small containers, with the rest of the activity supplies, next.

4. Fill any crevices with thin or small objects, such as the garden containers, the trowel, and duster.

5. On top, place any soft or malleable items, such as the apron and towel.

6. Secure the container's lid and label the outside of the box.

# Upcycle

By 2050, landfill waste is expected to increase by about 70 percent as the global population grows.

ANY PREVENTABLE ACTION in trying to stop goods from going to waste is much needed. If you ask me, I would rather upcycle than recycle. Although both processes are extremely necessary to reduce waste ending up in landfills, the found-and-rescued factor of having an upcycled useful product that comes with a certain history always gets me. A history that serves as a backbone or frame for its new future, not to mention less energy and fewer resources are involved in its creation.

In an upcycling project, the old, used, or unwanted product is transformed into a new one—sometimes, with little resemblance of what its original function was. In gardening, upcycling is a common practice.

Before I even consider donating, recycling, or, if there is no other option, putting something into the garbage, I ask myself how this artifact can be used in my garden or another part of the house. Here is where creativity kicks in, and Pinterest becomes one of your best reference tools.

A Google search alone shows more than eighty-four million results when you look for the term "upcycling." As we look for sustainable solutions to do our part in saving the planet, upcycling is becoming one of the go-to responses of eco-minded people who also appreciate the creativity and uniqueness that upcycling brings to the equation.

In a European study about the appeal of upcycled products to consumers, the researchers offered a new perspective on why upcycled products are viewed favorably and how creative perceptions are formed. They found that the more distance between the new outcome of an object from its old functionality, the more creatively the project is perceived, and its appeal is greater in comparison to other upcycled products used in similar capacities from their old life.

Rescuing an old table from a pile of garbage and giving it a new life with some paint is still a sustainable action, but it won't be perceived to be as creative as repurposing the same old table into a love seat with the addition of a back, fresh paint, and a couple of comfortable cushions to place in a garden corner.

According to the research results, it is relevant to understand how consumers perceive creativity because it will dictate future behavior, like whether or not to purchase a product. They also suggest that these insights should be used to market and enhance the upcycled outcome while promoting sustainable products.

I enjoy taking the time to repurpose objects. I have found used treasures in people's front yards, recycling bins, and garbage containers. Going through secondhand store inventory is one of my favorite hobbies.

Sometimes, I go with a specific need in mind but, most of the time, I just let the object speak to me, and then ask myself if, eventually, it can be repurposed and whether I have the time and resources to work on it in a reasonable time frame (less than six months), and whether it will be fun. I take all these questions into consideration before I buy or rescue something to bring into my home.

The next few projects are examples and an invitation for you to start asking yourself if the objects you already own are being used at their maximum proposed functionality (before you start to consider getting rid of them) or if they could be more useful for other purposes.

Start exploring your home, neighborhood, or even workplace (ask first before taking anything with you) and let your imagination fly.

When you have a potential upcycling project in your hands, remember that you don't need to have all the answers at that precise moment. Most of the time, I let the idea, and object, marinate for a few days before I finally lay down a plan. In the meantime, I gather tools and materials that could be helpful in enhancing the outcome.

Sometimes, I keep objects thinking they will be used in certain parts of the garden and they end up indoors, serving a more practical function.

When it comes to potential gardening projects that will help the Earth's well-being, waste no time. **V**

## Self-Assessment Time

Do a self-assessment to see how upcycling is part of your life by answering these questions.

1. What would you rather do: Recycle or repurpose? Why?

   ---------------------------------------------------------

   ---------------------------------------------------------

2. If you´re into upcycling, what type of objects do you repurpose the most?

   ---------------------------------------------------------

   ---------------------------------------------------------

3. Where do you look for potential artifacts to repurpose? (Second-hand stores, family attics, your home.)

   ---------------------------------------------------------

   ---------------------------------------------------------

4. How fast do you upcycle a newfound object? (Within a day, weeks to months, more than a year.)

   ---------------------------------------------------------

   ---------------------------------------------------------

5. Usually, why do you repurpose objects? (To keep for yourself, gift to someone, or sell.)

   ---------------------------------------------------------

   ---------------------------------------------------------

6. What are three objects you look forward to repurposing this month, if any?

   ---------------------------------------------------------

   ---------------------------------------------------------

# Candelabra
# Plant
# Holder

Turn a pair of iron leaf-shaped
candelabra into succulent holders.

## PROJECT DESCRIPTION

In the Walt Disney Pictures blockbuster animated movie *Beauty and the Beast*, the candelabrum character, Lumiere (French for "light"), is characterized as a kind, gracious host, and key in helping Belle and the Beast fall in love. The movie was based on the 1740 French story *La Belle et la Bête* by Gabrielle-Suzanne Barbot de Villeneuve.

A couple years after the animated movie came out, international rock star Meat Loaf recorded the romantic hit song "I'd Do Anything for Love (But I Won't Do That)" and launched a music video for the theme based on the stories of *Beauty and the Beast* and *The Phantom of the Opera*. Romantic indeed!

A lot of candelabra were used in the video. At that time I was a teenager, seventeen or eighteen, and a very romantic one, attracted to storylines about love, drama, and impossible romances. Of course, I would associate a candelabrum with a romantic love scene. Although, having one close by is highly recommended, if not to enhance your love life, at least as a source of light in case of a power outage.

As soon as I saw this pair of candelabra in the secondhand shop, I knew how I wanted to use them. Not as candleholders, their original purpose, but as plant stands. I know it's not a new idea, but like many romantic storylines, it's an idea that never gets old. Each candelabrum had a candleholder surrounded by three leaf-shaped railings, perfect for a small planter.

I decided on succulents (*Sedum adolphii*) and terra-cotta planters, but any small houseplant would fit perfectly. For the transformational part, I chose spray paint; olive green

These candelabra were meant to be together.

for the candelabra and watermelon pink for the planter's exterior. As I wanted to place it on a small table in the living room, I wanted the colors to coordinate with the indoor garden shed I have near the sofa (see "Indoor Garden Shed," page 116).

### About *Sedum adolphii*

*Sedum adolphii* is a succulent plant also known as golden sedum or golden glow. It can grow up to 12 inches (30 cm) tall and 24 inches (60 cm) wide. It likes sunny spots but can thrive in bright indirect light, too. The plant's small green rosettes are formed with pointy oviform-shaped leaves, which you can use to propagate the plant, as well as the stem. The leaf tip and border are red. As with many succulent varieties, this one is drought-tolerant but needs to be watered when the soil is dry. The plant can survive to temperatures as low as 20°F [-7°C]. Use a sandy soil mix appropriate for cacti.

## Materials used in this project

- Two 13-inch (32.5 cm)-high iron candelabra
- Two 4½-inch (11 cm)-wide terra-cotta planters
- Removable adhesive tape
- Drop cloths
- Gloves
- Mask
- Safety glasses
- Watermelon pink spray paint
- Olive green spray paint
- Two 4-inch (10 cm) succulents (*Sedum adolphii*)
- Potting soil appropriate for cacti and succulents

## Preparing the container

1. Dust off the candelabra and terra-cotta planters.
2. Use tape to cover any areas of the planters that you don't want to paint.
3. Cover the areas where you'll be painting with drop cloths, and place the planters on the cloths.
4. Wearing gloves, a mask, and safety glasses, spray the uncovered areas of the planters with the watermelon pink paint and let them dry.
5. Paint the candelabra with the olive green paint and let them dry.
6. Transplant the succulents into the terra-cotta planters, add new soil, and water the plants. Let the containers drain before placing them on the candelabra.
7. Place and secure your new candelabra plant holders in an area that receives bright indirect light.

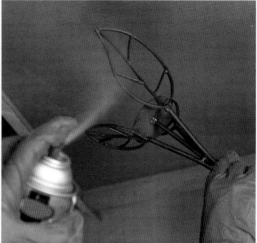

## PROJECT DESCRIPTION

For more than a year, I had an old tire rolling from one part of the garden to another. At first, it was in my car's trunk, but it was an unpractical situation because of its size, so I decided to roll it into the garden. I cringed every time I saw it, but I felt better knowing that it was one less tire contributing to a bigger environmental problem.

I also knew a garden project was coming soon.

We all have seen tires, especially old ones, recycled and repurposed for all kinds of projects, such as flooring in recreational facilities or used to create retaining walls. And in agricultural and gardening projects, their uses are numerous—from the agricultural practice of terracing to garden containers, borders, and sitting areas, to name a few. And, yes, I contemplated a few of these options for my garden.

In my quest to attract more wildlife into my garden, particularly urban birds, I installed a birdbath under a 15-foot (4.5 m)-tall soursop tree (*Annona muricata*), which resulted in a hit—for the birds and for me. Believe me when I tell you that once you install this project, including a bird feeder, your garden breaks will last longer. For the birdbath, I repurposed a Japanese ceramic bowl that I bought in a secondhand shop and placed it on a metal stand. That's it!

Based on this gratifying experience, I decided to try to replicate it in other parts of the garden, and the old tire was perfect for this purpose.

When I look at the birdbath from the laundry window or from the healing corner nearby (see "Healing Nook," page 94), I no longer cringe when I see the old tire—instead, I long for more time to enjoy how life is transformed in my little backyard spot.

◁ Repurpose an old tire into a practical birdbath base.

The new, and bigger, birdbath was placed in a cool area near my green hedge of lantana (*Lantana*) and pennyroyal (*Mentha pulegium*). A few herb containers surrounding the stand were protected from heavy winds and the harsh tropical sun, no matter the season.

(*left*) Of course, repurposing the tire also included a transformational look. After cleaning the tire inside and out, I painted it a bone-white color. (*right*) Then, I decorated the tire with jute cord whose thickness fit perfectly into the tire's treads, contributing to the camouflage effect. It was ready to be used as a dish holder.

For the birdbath, I used a 19-inch (48 cm) plastic terra-cotta-colored saucer, 2 inches (5 cm) deep, placed over a plastic lid, which fit perfectly into the 21-inch (53 cm) tire opening. As for the plastic trash container, I used it for two main purposes: storage and a secure stand. The container had two handles on each side, which helped to keep the tire, now base, in place at a safe height.

## Materials used for this project

- One 26-inch (66 cm) old tire
- Drop cloths
- Gloves (optional)
- Mask (optional)
- Bone-white fast-drying enamel (oil) paint
- Paintbrush
- Weather-resistant glue
- Jute cord
- One 21 × 20½-inch (53 × 51 cm)-diameter plastic container, with lid
- One 19-inch (48 cm) plastic terra-cotta-colored saucer, 1 or 2 inches (2.5 or 5 cm) deep
- Potted herbs and/or flowering plants

## Preparing the container

1. Clean the tire well inside and out and let dry.

2. Cover the area where you'll be painting with a drop cloth. Place the tire on the drop cloth and paint the top and sides of the tire. Let dry completely before turning it over and painting the other side. Let dry.

3. Once the paint is dry, fill the tire treads with a small amount of glue. Insert the jute rope around the tire, into the treads. The amount of cord you'll need will depend on the kind of tire you're using. Let the glue dry.

4. Place the plastic container in the designated area and fill it with garden materials and accessories that you do not use on a daily basis, then lay the tire on top.

5. Turn the container's lid upside-down and place it over the tire's hole (it should be a few inches bigger). Place the plastic saucer on top of the lid.

6. Fill the saucer with fresh water, no more than 2 inches (5 cm) deep. The birds will find the water.

7. Place herbs and flowering plants around the standing base to hide or camouflage the container. To encourage birds to come to the new birdbath area, add a bird feeder nearby.

8. Add fresh water to the bath, at least every two days, and keep the bath (plastic saucer) clean.

For the birdbath, repurpose a plastic trash container and a plastic terracotta-colored saucer, 2 inches (5cm) deep. The plastic container will hold the repurposed tire, on top of it will go the inverted container lid, and lastly the saucer filled with water for the birds.

# Indoor Garden Shed

## PROJECT DESCRIPTION

Extra storage is always welcome in my home, especially because I have been gardening for a long time. Eventually, you, too, will realize the importance of keeping things tidy and accessible (no matter the space) to make sure you spend more time gardening instead of exhausting yourself looking for your gardening tools and materials.

Whether you garden indoors, outdoors, or both, aside from a flat surface and a comfortable chair, you will need a safe space for keeping your unused planters, tools, gadgets, soil bags, fertilizers, and garden accessories.

Usually, the amount of space dedicated to storage is determined by the size of your gardening projects and the time you allot for them. Of course, you will also need to keep an eye on your storage space, otherwise, you could end up with a garden center.

As I have mentioned before, I live in the terrace apartment of a walk-up building. I have a front yard and a backyard, but to get from one to the other I need to cross my living room, dining room, and kitchen area. So, you can imagine the amount of dirt I leave along the way every time I go from point A to point B.

To maximize time, and reduce fatigue, and dirt, too, I decided to distribute all my gardening tools and materials properly in key spots around the house, from the backyard and front terrace to my home office. Because I have plants everywhere, it's a practical strategy for easy access where and when they might be needed.

I like to keep most of the soil bags in the backyard, but I also have a container filled with soil in the front yard. It's convenient to have

duplicate small tools, such as pruners, watering cans, close by, too.

An important issue to think about when repurposing indoor areas for garden storage is how to blend them with the rest of your home's furniture. You want your family to know they still have a living room and dining table to use and enjoy. Practicality and functionality are even more important when your space is limited and buying a new cabinet or garden shed isn't an option.

Look around your home to identify potential storage areas or accessories you already have that are probably being underutilized. It could be an empty drawer, a kitchen corner cabinet, or baskets piled up in the closet. If you are certain that nobody will miss them, start

◁ Transform an ordinary basket stand into colorful storage for your gardening tools and materials.

the upcycling process to upgrade your garden lifestyle.

This is what I did with a wooden stand and a wicker basket. Both items were around my home for some time, in the kitchen and other rooms, and always ended up being used as lost-and-found containers, holding one or two items we'd deal with later— and suddenly those items were impossible to find, because they were buried under a thousand more.

This time, I decided to repurpose them together as indoor garden storage in the living room, near the front-yard garden and I decorated the items to blend in with the rest of the furniture. My new-found storage is perfect for holding basic tools, small planters, and other garden materials in small quantities—all necessary elements in case of an after-dark gardening session or when you just want to garden while watching TV.

I went online for some inspiration and decided on the basket painting trend with matching round containers to store some products safely.

## Materials used in this project

- Basket stand
- Two 12-inch-long × 7½-inch-wide (30.5 × 19 cm) wicker baskets, that will fit on the stand
- One 16-inch (40.6 cm) top-diameter wicker basket, that will sit next to the stand on a pot caddy
- One 16-inch (40.6 cm) round plastic terra-cotta tray (optional)
- One 14-inch (35.6 cm) round plastic terra-cotta caddy (optional)
- Towel
- Drop cloths
- Bone-white fast-drying oil paint
- Medium-size paintbrush
- Removable adhesive tape in different sizes
- Gloves
- Mask
- Safety glasses
- Matte seaside green spray paint
- Gloss watermelon pink spray paint
- Jute cord
- Plastic hooks
- Round plastic containers
- Removable adhesive chalkboard labels to label the contents of each container (optional)

## Preparing the container

1. Remove the two baskets (originally there were three) from the stand. Clean the baskets and stand with a moist towel and let them dry. Follow the same process with the single wicker basket.

2. Cover the area where you'll be painting the stand with drop cloths and place the stand on it. Paint the stand with bone-white oil paint and let it dry for at least 1 hour.

3. Place tape on all the baskets to create simple designs and delineate where paint will be and where it will not be sprayed on. Wearing gloves, a mask, and safety glasses, spray the baskets with the matte and gloss spray paints as desired. Let dry.

4. Attached the baskets to the stand using the jute.

5. Place a few plastic hooks on each side of the stand on which to hang tools.

6. Secure the wicker basket handles using the jute.

Adding the caddy facilitates moving the basket once it is filled with heavy materials.

If you make a similar project, use the plastic tray as a lid for the wicker basket, and place a small plant on top. Of course, use the tray to contain any mess when gardening indoors.

Use smaller plastic containers to store materials like preserved moss and stones. Label them with the contents of each container.

# Propagation Wall Station

## PROJECT DESCRIPTION

Plant propagation is a skill that can be learned and mastered. It's also a fun way to experiment and increase the number of plants in your indoor or outdoor garden. You can multiply the *verdura* in your life using seeds (sexual reproduction) or by using cuttings from several parts of the plant (asexual reproduction) depending on the type of cultivar.

The success of your propagation method will depend on several important factors, like the quality of the seeds or cuttings you use and the environmental conditions that influence the seed's germination or whether the cuttings take root.

Of course, we are part this equation, too. If you are not paying attention to the propagation process—overdoing or minimizing some of your gardening duties—the potential success of having a healthy plant will diminish, bringing with it frustration and disappointment.

In horticulture therapy, propagation activities are used to support a variety of treatment for people with a specific diagnosis or who are participating in an overall wellness program. For example, a vocational program focused on teaching functional and transferable skills would include instruction on several propagation techniques along with other horticultural skills that would then allow the person to use the new information for employment opportunities or volunteering services. The person will also use these new skills for their personal well-being, whether to grow food or landscape plants to beautify the home, as well.

Experimenting with propagation, and succeeding in its mastery, contributes to all aspects of our well-being. It increases self-confidence and self-esteem; we can teach others what we have learned and we learn to slow down and focus. We are more observant of changes, like the growth of new roots, buds, or leaves, which help keep us moving forward with a growth mentality.

A few days after Hurricane Maria hit Puerto Rico in 2017, propagating plants from seeds or cuttings was an activity I used for coping with the painful circumstances after the devastating storm. I incorporated the process into my daily routine; the germination or watching a plant rooting in water, in just a few days, helped me keep my focus, cope with stress and anxiety, and, most importantly, gave me hope and purpose.

Repurposing a hanging shower caddy into a propagation station is a fun and practical project, environmentally friendly, and decorative, too. All bases are covered!

The rusty accessory may not work anymore for my bathroom, but it certainly is a great addition to my potting area or any other part of the house with good lighting and ventilation. With a little spray paint, the new propagation caddy holds a few clear-glass containers. Yes, you guessed it—empty clear wine bottles and sauce jars.

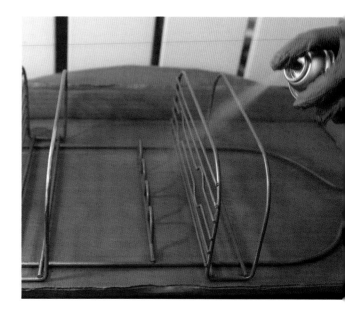

◁ Turn an old rusty metal hanging shower caddy into a wall propagation station.

## Using Your Propagation Wall Station

- Choose a location with bright indirect sunlight to hang your station.
- Use clear containers to facilitate checking for mosquito larvae; if found, change the water and clean the container before reinserting the plant.
- Use young stem cuttings, 4 to 5 inches (10 to 13 cm) long.
- Change the water at least once a week.
- Don't submerge leaves in the water; they will rot and create harmful bacteria.

I use a removable adhesive chalkboard label to add the name of each cultivar.

The vessels are great for propagating herbs, houseplants, and soft wood cuttings. Pothos, hibiscus, lavender, and basil are some of my most successful accomplishments, and ones I'm proudest of, using just water to root them.

Being able to see the beautiful growing roots will enhance your gardening space and serve as a motivational reminder to keep going. Placing the propagation caddy on the wall helps maximize the space and is an icebreaker for social interactions with friends and family interested in gardening.

If you're doing a similar project, make sure to adjust it to your location and circumstances. You should be able to reach it in a comfortable way and secure it to the wall, as it will hold fragile containers. Any kitchen or bathroom accessory or piece of furniture, such as a rolling cart or cabinet, can serve as a propagation station as long it can hold your upcycled propagation jars safely. If not on the wall, place it on a stool or table, but personalize it using your creativity.

## Materials used in this project

- Drop cloths
- Olive green spray paint
- One 11½ × 24-inch (29 × 60 cm) metal shower caddy
- Gloves
- Mask
- Safety glasses
- Drilling tools and materials (optional)
- 7 clear-glass containers (such as 4 small empty wine bottles and 3 [15-ounce, or 440 ml] empty sauce jars)
- Removable adhesive chalkboard labels
- Stem cuttings

## Preparing the container

1. Cover the area where you'll be painting with drop cloths. Place the caddy on the cloths and, wearing gloves, a mask, and safety glasses, spray it with olive green spray paint. Let dry.

2. Prepare the wall, or other area, and do the drilling or other installation labor where you'll install the caddy while it dries. Hang or position the caddy once dry.

3. Clean and label the glass containers.

4. Fill the containers with clean water and add the stem cuttings, then place the containers in the caddy.

5. Plan the type of planter, and the location for it, once the plant has rooted sufficiently for its next step in the propagation process.

# Swinging Planter

Turn a metal fruit basket into a fun and memorable container for plants. Placing a saucer under the container basket prevents any liquid splatter when watering.

To facilitate the gardening process, I place the basket on a flat surface and use a saucer for stabilization.

## PROJECT DESCRIPTION

When I was a kid, I loved the flying swing ride or swing carousel (and I still do) better than any other ride as part of the entertainment of *fiestas patronales*, or local municipal festivities, or the seasonal amusement parks I used to visit with my family, and, as I grew older, with friends.

The ride was basic—you sat on a seat suspended from the rotating top of the carousel. The seats had a security bar at waist height to prevent you from falling out. Some of these rides had a tilting top, which made them more exciting, and as soon as the machine started moving, you grabbed the metal chains suspending the chairs as hard as you could and flew along with it. I had no control at all, except for the strength of my arms trying not to let go of the chains and the effort to keep my rear on

the seat while my body flew 15 feet (4.5 m) off the ground.

The best thing about the five-minute bird's-eye-view ride was the event's landscape: the sea of people gathering around and amusing themselves on other rides; the bright lights, loud music, undisputable popcorn scent, and the cold breeze hitting my face. Don't get me wrong, that ride was scary, but the liberating feeling of being up there as a bird was thrilling and exciting. I was grateful every time I touched the ground but eager to go back.

So, the next closest way to feel as though I was flying was on the swings or hammocks at home. At my house, we always had a hammock hanging on the patio. I used it to play, rest, and read, and, yes, to compete with my brothers to see who could go higher and faster.

Unlike traditional swings in the park or hanging on the strong branches of a tree, cloth hammocks are easy to fold, less complicated to hang, and you can take them everywhere with you.

In Puerto Rico, it is common to see hammock sale posts on the side of the freeway or in souvenir shops. They are part of our Puerto Rican culture and heritage and a present-day reminder of our Indigenous ancestors, the *Taíno* culture, who used hammocks for multiple purposes in their society, beyond resting, as we mostly use them today. I even have one in my closet waiting to be hung.

Whether a hammock or a swing, both are great features to add to our homes, even better if you have an open space like a garden in which to put it. These accessories are fun and great contributors to our good health, too.

Taking a break from the daily work routine for a few minutes on a swing can help us relax and refocus before going back to what we were doing, in a better mood. It also helps us go from sedentary to movement, because we have to push ourselves, literally, to have a great swing. Unless we have someone who can give us the first push, we have to use our lower body (legs) to propel us and our upper body (arms) to grab the hangers or whatever keeps us from falling, as well as to keep us going in the air. This action alone makes us concentrate on the present, forgetting, at least while we're in the air, any source of stress and anxiety.

And also, for some of us, using a swing or hammock nowadays, in any outdoor circumstance, could represent an opportunity to engage with more positive experiences, tap into beloved childhood memories, reconnect with nature, and feel restored mentally.

This next project reminds me of exactly how much fun I had as a kid and teenager on the neighborhood swings, my parents' hammock, or up on the swinging carousels. Although the plants won't swing as high or fast, securing them in their peculiar container is important for a smooth ride that will help them thrive.

This is a garden project you can replicate easily as hanging fruit baskets are easy to find in stores. I bought the one I use in this project in a secondhand store, and knew immediately that I wanted to use it as a plant container.

Like any fruit basket, this project will look amazing on a kitchen counter. If you have good, bright lighting, you can use it for some of your favorite herbs, or for interesting houseplants like I do. I combined three beautiful plants: Zumba begonia (*Begonia rex* 'Zumba'), which reminds me of the top of a swinging carousel, the intriguing heart fern, *Hemionitis arifolia*, and a beetle peperomia, *Peperomia quadrangularis*.

Separately, these three plants like bright indirect light and rich moist soil, not puddled. Because they are elevated and planted within a coconut coir sheet, the soil will dry faster than if it were in a regular container. So, it needs more frequent watering than most of my other houseplants.

As a finishing detail, I used the hook of the basket station for hanging bananas and other similar fruits and hung a ceramic rainbow and cloud pendant from it, a reminder of how fun it was trying to fly into the sky with every swing.

## Materials used in this project

- Drop cloths
- Gloves
- Mask
- Safety glasses
- Olive green spray paint
- 1 large chrome metal hanging fruit basket with hanger
- Scissors
- Coconut coir liner for the basket
- Three small 4- or 5-inch (10 or 13 cm) houseplants, such as Zumba begonia, *Begonia rex* 'Zumba', beetle peperomia, *Peperomia quadrangularis*, and heart fern, *Hemionitis arifolia*.
- Potting soil
- Garden spade
- Decorative item (optional)

## Preparing the container

1. Cover the area where you'll be painting with drop cloths.

2. Wearing gloves, a mask, and safety glasses, paint the fruit basket and hanger with several layers of spray paint. Let dry between layers.

3. Cut the coconut liner to fit the basket and place it in the basket.

4. Fill the bottom of the coconut liner with potting soil, then transplant the houseplants, starting with the thriller (heart fern), then filler (begonia), and, finally, spiller (peperomia), into it, adding more soil to cover the plants' roots.

5. Attach the hanger to its designated area and secure the basket to it.

6. Add a decorative element to the hanger, if desired.

▷ Rainbow and cloud clay pendant—a gift from a dear and talented friend, Puerto Rican ceramist Sylvia Colón Inglés.

# Grow into Your Own

Any garden project is an amazing opportunity to reflect on and express your gardening lifestyle.

IF YOU HAVE BEEN gardening for a long time, I'm certain you have noticed changes over time, but also characteristics or patterns that repeat. If you're just beginning, growing into your style is a beautiful process that never ends.

Know this, just like gardens, there are no two gardening lifestyles that are alike. What you bring is unique and worth sharing with others.

For some people, it may appear that their style comes easily. Don't waste your precious energy on what you think you haven't figured out yet. It will come. The important thing is, once you become aware of who you are and what you need, and how gardening can benefit all areas of your life, embrace each opportunity, and share them with family and friends. They will be the first to respect and encourage your nature breaks. Their understanding and support, too, will translate into more confidence and satisfaction.

Through our gardening lifestyle, even when we're not aware of it, we express who we are and where we are, physically, emotionally, and mentally. Yes, economically, too, but having money doesn't always mean having everything needed.

Our gardening lifestyle carries our individual cultural backgrounds and our creative identity; and as with the home garden, it's expected to change, or at least adjust, over

time. Each gardening project should represent who we are at a certain moment in time—from taste, attitudes, and habits to values, passions, and preferences. It would be ideal that it leads us, each time, closer to our best state of well-being.

Any adjustments in our gardening lifestyle come more easily when we consider our life circumstances today, and in the future. Besides knowledge, skills, and space, our gardening lifestyle should reflect how much time we have available to garden as well as our mobility, strength, and stamina.

In my case, I use my garden and gardening projects to relax, experiment, and flow (even work-related projects). It took me time to align what I thought I wanted with what I needed. Once I got it, I haven't stopped talking about it, and in this, I found even more confidence and inspiration to keep going.

In the article "Healthy Lifestyle Through Home Gardening: The Art of Sharing," Dr. Sothy Eng and colleagues state that inspiration is a key factor (along with skills and knowledge) in creating and keeping a home garden. They gather from the literature that people interested in gardening "need to be inspired to have the desire to create and care for a garden in the first place." This can apply, too, when it comes to defining our gardening lifestyle. You come up with an invisible filter or guides that somehow end up comforting you and, without planning, become a beacon for others. We not only share the produce of a harvest, but also resources, experiences, and stories that connect us to each other more tightly. Family, friends, and strangers become our sounding board. As we give to others, we also nurture our self-esteem, strengthening confidence, and building healthy communities through gardening endeavors.

Eng et al., compare gardens to "time capsules" that contain past memories, nature familiarity, and social networks. Home gardens and gardening projects, in beds or containers, hold part of our gardening lifestyle history, too. They are the result of our physical, emotional, and mental states at a certain moment.

This section is meant for you to take these project ideas and flip them, imprint them with your style to reflect where you're coming from and where you want to lead your life, in gardening and in general.

In this section, you will find project ideas that inspire you to display who you are, grow botanical gifts, and continue to build your legacy through the plants you love. ∨

## Self-Assessment Time

Do a self-assessment to help you grow into your gardening lifestyle by answering these questions:

1. How much time do I have for gardening?

   ----------------------------------------

   ----------------------------------------

2. How do I describe my mobility?

   ----------------------------------------

   ----------------------------------------

3. How big is my gardening space? Is it outdoors, indoors, or both?

   ----------------------------------------

   ----------------------------------------

4. What are my gardening preferences? Ornamental and/or edibles?

   ----------------------------------------

   ----------------------------------------

5. How are my physical abilities to do certain gardening tasks? Do I need assistance with some?

   ----------------------------------------

   ----------------------------------------

6. Besides gardening, what other things do I enjoy spending time doing?

   ----------------------------------------

   ----------------------------------------

   ----------------------------------------

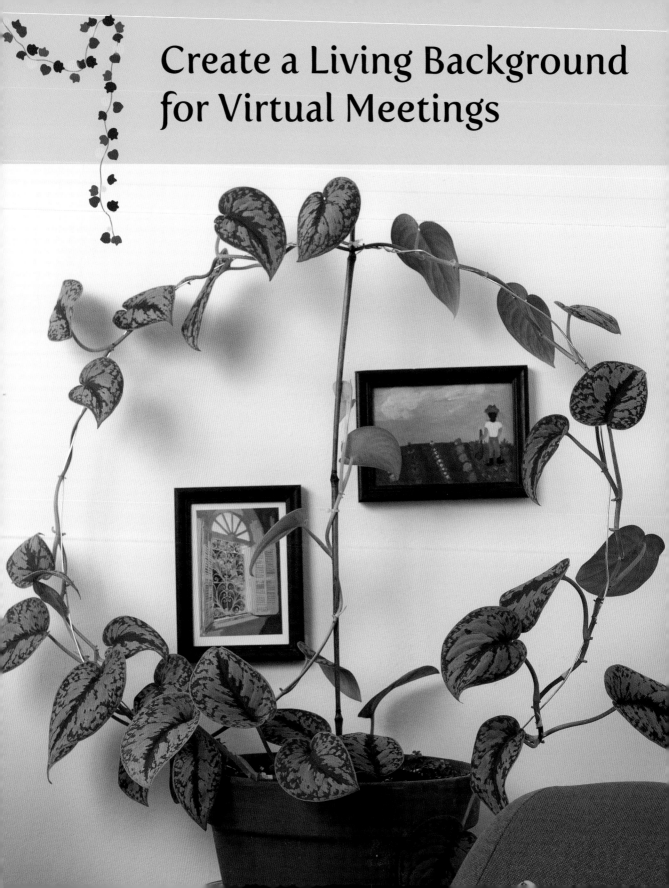

# Create a Living Background for Virtual Meetings

## PROJECT DESCRIPTION

Nowadays, virtual meetings are part of our daily routine. From work to social gatherings, they help us stay in touch, connected, and familiar despite distances.

When we turn on the camera, we have the opportunity to build intimacy with others, letting them "see," through the screen, who we are. Yes, our physical appearance, if they are not acquaintances, but also our moods, tastes, and aspirations before we even unmute ourselves.

According to the virtual meeting platform Zoom, 63 percent of their users prefer taking calls with their camera on. (I'm one of them). Forty three percent of those who decide to go with a real background, instead of a virtual one, said "they cleaned only the part of the room visible on camera."

I try to have the whole room clean and tidy just in case of a quick switch of backgrounds. Speaking of which, when I'm giving a virtual workshop or attending a regular meeting, people ask me regularly if the background is real, and I say yes proudly.

Most of the time, I receive compliments and questions about what's going on behind me, and you will, too, when you turn on the camera and share your personal green scene with the world.

This is a great way to socialize—to break the ice or warm up any virtual room before everyone goes straight to business. The natural environment humanizes us, and when we see plants as part of the picture, we get

I make sure people know my interests as soon as see what is behind me: plants, books, and art/crafts.

comfortable, relax, and open up. Suddenly, someone owns a similar plant and starts sharing their experience.

Sometimes, peeking into people's virtual background is like peeking into someone's garden—even a small area can amaze.

If you work from home but don't have a space you claim as a home office for your video conferences, but want to green-up an empty wall behind you, this transformational gardening project will do just that. And, the best part is, you won't have to worry about people or pets popping into your frame if you don't want them to. Because you're going to be adding plants, choose those that can thrive with the natural lighting of your space.

You may already have one of its kin, but if not, it is easy to find in any garden center or garden boutique. Instead of using a moss pole for the plant to climb on, I made a round trellis using wire hangers attached to a bamboo stick.

A trellis is a support structure for the plant. Instead of letting the plant just hang or trail

◁ I created a real, natural background for virtual meetings—tangling a houseplant vine around a round trellis and other meaningful objects, like framed artwork, a hand-painted picture from my Aunt Wanda, and a postcard from my alma mater Universidad del Sagrado Corazón, made by Taller UNA.

### About *Scindapsus pictus*

This tropical plant enjoys temperatures between 65°F and 85°F (18°C and 29°C) and thrives in bright indirect light. Compared to other varieties of the Arum (*Araceae*) family, this pant is a slow grower. Its foliage is gray to silver variegation.

For this project, I used one of my favorite go-to plants, the 'Silver Satin' pothos (*Scindapsus pictus*).

As part of the composition, I added a small piece of framed art to fill the center of the plant trellis.

The background should not be a distraction to the meeting. Because the trellis is the focal point, I complement it with other objects. When personalizing the space, add a few of your favorite books, smaller plants, or personal memorabilia.

along the floor, you train it around the trellis. Adding a climbing plant to your background will help you stand out in any virtual meeting.

The best scenario is that, after you finish your work and shut down your computer, the space blends in with the rest of the room.

This is a project you can do in a day, or you can divide it into several parts over a weekend with the help of family and friends: the gardening, choosing and framing the art, fixing up furniture, and then putting all together.

## Virtual Meeting Tips

1. Position your computer screen 16 to 30 inches (40 to 75 cm) from your eyes, with the top of your screen level with, or slightly below, your eyes.

2. Use a box or a few books to raise the screen when using a laptop.

3. Remove anything from view that seems too busy or too big.

4. Wear bright, solid colors to stand out.

5. Leave at least 3 feet (90 cm) of space between your chair and your background.

6. Use as much natural light as possible; if needed, use a selfie ring or LED lamp to reduce shadows and enhance your appearance.

## Materials used in this project

- 2 wire hangers
- One 24-inch (60 cm)-long, ½-inch (1 cm)-thick bamboo stick
- 1 'Silver Satin' pothos (*Scindapsus pictus*)
- One 12 × 8-inch (30 × 20 cm) round terra-cotta pot
- Potting soil
- Hand spade
- Preserved moss in forest green
- Favorite framed art pieces
- Removable adhesive hooks for hanging
- Cable ties to secure the wire to the bamboo stick
- Metal stand
- Desk
- Chair and pillow

## Preparing the space

1. Create the wire trellis with the hangers and bamboo stick by loosening the top part of the hangers and straightening them as much as possible. Then bend the wires into a round shape (use performance work gloves for this), twisting the ends together to keep the circular form. Place the bamboo stick in the middle of the round shape and secure the wire to it using two cable ties—one on top of the stick and another a few inches (cm) up from the bottom. Insert the base of the bamboo stick into the pot. Let the base of the trellis's circle rest on the pot's rim.

2. Transplant the pothos into the pot and wrap the vines around the wire trellis. Place moss on top of the soil as a decorative mulch.

3. Choose the art and other decorative accessories you'll incorporate into the view. Hang them in place.

4. Select and/or fix the furniture you'll use.

5. Put together your real background.

## PROJECT DESCRIPTION

If death catches me in the garden, which I really hope it does, it will likely find me barefoot, with a damp cloth, some sort of harvest scattered by one side and sharp shears on the other, while my body phases peacefully to the next stage of my life.

For many of us, it's difficult to discuss our passing, even though as gardeners we are reminded constantly by our plants that dying is another natural process, as is germination and procreation. Somehow, gardening is the discreet and patient teacher, always available, to help us prepare and accept the fact of letting go.

Unfortunately, going through life denying what is natural for all of us has the potential to minimize our desired legacy as well as add to the pain of our loved ones who have to deal directly with our physical passing as well as figuring out what to do with the possessions we leave behind.

Author and psychoanalyst Sue Stuart-Smith shared in her book *The Well-Gardened Mind* that many studies have pointed out that our brain processes death "as something that happens to other people." Yes, we're aware that someday we will die, but not in our decided near future. Stuart-Smith explains that by not accepting how death is directly related to us, we protect ourselves from "overwhelming anxiety," even if this means living in constant denial. "If we think about dying too much it interferes with living, but if we never think about death, we remain perilously unprepared."

It's not just enough to talk about and express your wishes for when you're no longer in this world. Generally, we have to involve legal counsel to follow up and make things happen according to our country's law regarding heirs, asset division, and particular wishes.

If you don't leave written instructions, such as a last will and testament, your assets, including your gardening possessions, will be inventoried and executed according to the laws in your state or country. By no means am I offering legal advice, much less telling you what to do. I just want to share with you (what I'm already starting to do) to consider some potential ideas on how to begin categorizing beloved gardening objects; to start thinking about who might be interested in having and using them for the greater good, and even leaving a clear guide to a loved one on how to proceed with your garden legacy once you can't anymore.

The most important thing to know is what you own, and if necessary, have written proof of it. You can't give away or leave an inheritance that isn't yours. Specifically, regarding garden-related things, start by doing a general inventory of all your garden goods, from plants to tools, at your home or any other property you own. Of course, the bigger and more possessions you own, the more details you need to get into, with its own particularities.

Give to this project a positive and cheerful connotation. Focus on what you have built or grown through time, on how grateful you are, and on how this organization process will help you continue planning for more meaningful gardening experiences, with the peace of mind that, someday, other people will be able to enjoy part of it because of your preparedness. Also, this is a great opportunity to ask friends and family to help.

◁ Keep your *verdura* alive for generations to come.

## Use these five general categories, to start organizing your garden assets:

**1. Plant collection:** Include here beloved plants that are either potted or in garden beds. This could be roses, orchids, or a palm collection, or potted begonias or succulents. Start organizing the list by variety, preparing labels, and even writing down specifications. Ask family or friends whether they are interested in keeping some of your plants. Also, reach out to plant societies and become familiar with their protocols for receiving plant donations. Leave written instructions to family members regarding contacts and formal procedures.

List of my plant collection categories and people or organizations who might be interested in them:

------------------------------------------------

------------------------------------------------

------------------------------------------------

------------------------------------------------

------------------------------------------------

------------------------------------------------

**2. Gardening books:** You can organize your gardening books by language and subcategories, such as reference, fiction, topic, ornamentals, edibles, and kids' gardening activities. Think about friends and family, organizations, and public and private libraries who might be interested to create or grow their own gardening book collection. If donating your garden book collection is something you would like to do, start by creating a bibliography and become familiar with libraries' book donation formalities and conditions of acceptance.

List of my book collection categories and people or organizations who might be interested in them:

------------------------------------------------

------------------------------------------------

------------------------------------------------

------------------------------------------------

------------------------------------------------

------------------------------------------------

**3. Art collection:** In this category, you can include your favorite paintings, framed photographs, botanical prints, sculptures, garden installations, ceramics, and mixed-medium art. Everything garden related. Think about family and friends who might be interested in one or several of your art collection pieces. If you're interested in donating to an organization such as a botanical garden, library, university, or plant society, become acquainted with their donation acceptance policies and formalities.

List of my art collection categories and people or organizations who might be interested in them:

------------------------------------------------

------------------------------------------------

------------------------------------------------

------------------------------------------------

**4. Gardening tools and patio furnishings:**
Include here tools and accessories and patio
furniture in good condition and worth passing on.
Even hardscape can be reclaimed and put to good
use. Ask family and friends if they're interested,
or look into community organizations that
promote agriculture and gardening as part of their
programs. Get in contact and learn about their
donation acceptance protocols.

List of my tools, patio furnishings, and hardscape,
and people or organizations who might be
interested in them:

--------------------------------------------------------------

--------------------------------------------------------------

--------------------------------------------------------------

--------------------------------------------------------------

--------------------------------------------------------------

--------------------------------------------------------------

**5. Land, gardens, and buildings:** This category
has its own complications and formalities. It
is good to start thinking about what you'd like
to happen with your entire garden, farm, and
any buildings on it, and then seek the proper
legal counsel. There are many examples of
gardeners or garden lovers who have left their
land, gardens, and other properties as part of a
trust, foundation, or community organization to
ensure they're shared with the public or used for
other social good. There are garden exhibitions
and well-known garden shows, which after the
event, donate and, literally, move the gardens to
nongovernmental organizations.

List of my properties, gardens, and/or buildings,
and what I envision for them, and the people or
organizations who might be interested in fulfilling
this vision:

--------------------------------------------------------------

--------------------------------------------------------------

--------------------------------------------------------------

--------------------------------------------------------------

--------------------------------------------------------------

--------------------------------------------------------------

--------------------------------------------------------------

--------------------------------------------------------------

--------------------------------------------------------------

--------------------------------------------------------------

--------------------------------------------------------------

# Garden Art Installation
# in a Bonsai Dish

## PROJECT DESCRIPTION

Art has been part of my whole life. I was fortunate to be born into a family where all expressions of art were appreciated. My father, being a poet and a painter, hosted, along with my mother, small readings or art exhibitions at home or in local galleries.

I grew up surrounded by paintings hanging on every wall of the house, including in my room, and I have surrounded myself with art ever since. In almost every corner of my home, there are books, paintings, ceramics, and crafts along with the plants. Sometimes separate, or entangled together.

So, it was more than logical that I wanted, somehow, to take my indoor styling interests outdoors. And what better place for me to be inspired than Buffalo, New York.

In 2017, I was introduced formally to the garden tourism frenzy, thanks to Garden Walk Buffalo, a two-day event the last weekend of July, where thousands of people get the chance to visit private and public gardens around the city and peek into other garden lifestyles. A dream come true for someone who used to peek into people's gardens as a kid, a tendency that has never left me. The event also coincided with my first attendance at Garden Communicators International annual conference, held that year in the city of Buffalo. Garden tours, in person or virtually, are an intrinsic part of the conference.

During this well-known garden walk in the United States, and the biggest in its category, I got the chance to admire, touch, and smell incredible plants in such beautiful garden contexts. Also, I experienced the imagination and creativity of Buffalonians in using anything at their disposal to create artistic installations to complement or tell a story in their summer

◁ Create a showstopping art installation in a container to exhibit in your garden.

Inspired by amazing art experiences from my childhood, and as an adult, I created an art installation using a decorative home accent—a metal ant—found in a secondhand store and plants available in most garden centers, such as begonias and peperomias.

natural landscapes, whether in the back, front, or side yards.

For this garden project, I'm telling the story of a worker ant coming from the forest, carrying a leaf bigger than itself, who decides to stop on top of a mound, halfway through the journey, to take a garden break, contemplate the landscape, and appreciate from afar its colleagues, already downhill. It was easy for

me to come up with this fantastic short story because ants, of all the insects on the planet, are familiar and constants in our lives, and not just to gardeners.

In the book *Journey to the Ants*, the authors remind us of the ants' presence everywhere, minding their business as long as they aren't bothered. "Lean against a tree almost anywhere, and the first creature that crawls on you will probably be an ant. Stroll down a suburban sidewalk with your eyes fixed on the ground, counting the different kinds of animals you see. The ants will win hands down . . ." Consider this project an ode to the ant.

I used an oval plastic bonsai container, which is a shallow dish, to set up my imaginary landscape. What I like about this kind of container is that you have enough space to display a few plants and you can appreciate the content from different perspectives.

Luckily, the metal leaf reminded me of the form of a gorgeous *Begonia rex*, and which

would make an excellent representation of the forest area where our ant protagonist got its leaf. On the other hand, the *Peperomia caperata*, with its flowering spikes that look like antennae, was perfect to represent a group of ants carrying other leaves. The preserved moss was used to represent the ground, and the *Soleirolia soleirolii* would grow naturally to carpet the soil in the container.

According to studies, engaging in projects like this, which combine gardening and art-making activities, not only promotes creativity but also has therapeutic benefits to improve mental health—from experiencing positive mood changes to reducing depression and anxiety symptoms.

When in your journey exploring which art installation best suits your interests, do as the star of this story, take a garden break, enjoy your surroundings, and as you continue your path, ideas will come to you.

## Materials used in this project

- Drop cloths
- Gray latex paint
- Paintbrush
- One 22 × 16 × 4-inch (56 × 40 × 10 cm) oval plastic bonsai pot
- Gloves
- Mask
- Safety glasses
- 1 metal ant with leaf sculpture (ant's body is 6 × 2 inches [15 × 5 cm] and the leaf is 9 × 7 inches [23 × 18 cm])
- Olive green spray paint
- Scissors
- Garden fabric (weed barrier)
- One 6-inch (15 cm) begonia rex 'Fedor' (*Begonia rex*) plant
- Potting soil
- Hand spade
- One 5-inch (13 cm) silver ripple peperomia (*Peperomia caperata*) plant
- One 5-inch (13 cm) baby tears (*Soleirolia soleirolii*) plant
- Preserved moss

## Preparing the container

1. Cover the area where you'll be painting with drop cloths.

2. Paint the outside and inside of the plastic container, except for the bottom, with the gray latex paint. Let dry for a few hours before planting in it.

3. Wearing a mask, gloves, and safety glasses, paint the leaf of the ant with the spray paint. Let dry.

4. Cut the garden fabric to fit inside the bonsai container and cut off any excess fabric hanging over the rim.

5. Fill the container with potting soil, creating a small mound on one side of it. Transplant the begonia into the container and cover the plant's roots with more soil.

6. Fill the rest of the container with soil and transplant the peperomia at the edge of the container, opposite the begonia. Cover the plant's roots with soil.

7. Fill the container with soil in the center, leaving at least ½ inch (1 cm) of space near the rim.

8. Divide the baby tears into 2 or 3 portions and plant them at the edge of the small mound in the center of the container.

9. Using the preserved moss, layer it over the small mound around the begonia to create a visible border with the baby tears.

10. Place the metal ant in the center of the container. It should look like it's on top of the small mound.

# Display Your Favorite Plants

## PROJECT DESCRIPTION

What comes to mind when we hear the word "collection"? Is it paintings in a museum, cars parked in a garage, or dishes hung on the wall, reminders of a memorable trip to another country? Certainly, it can be anything.

A collection is the sum of objects gathered in one place for a particular purpose. This can be a study, comparison, exhibition, or simply a hobby.

Plant and garden people love to visit private and public exhibitions of plant collections. Whether it's in a botanical garden, a park, or a family backyard. In general, a plant collection can be dry specimens that are part of an herbarium, or a live bonsai, orchid, rose, or begonia collection growing in a garden plot or potted in containers. A plant collection can fit in one small room or, as I have witnessed, it can take a whole building.

I grew up surrounded by my parents' art collection. Mostly paintings. Because of my father's art background, it was normal for my brothers and me to see and hear him talk about his or a friend's collection. He would collect art from friends and also curate his own artwork for exhibitions. So, when I display my plant collection at home for my enjoyment, it's natural that I would borrow some tips from the art world to make them stand out.

If you're like me and many other plant parents, you love to talk about your plants and the small or big collection that you have, literally, grown over time. You show pictures, share caring tips, and even (for sure) pass down a propagated offspring of your favorite collection.

A fun way to share your plant passion, socialize differently, and even add more

◁ Showcase your plant collection and your dearest garden-related objects.

*verdura* to your life is by curating and displaying your or someone else's plant collection. And if you think you don't have enough interesting plants for a home exhibition, you can always create a collective with friends.

This plant project is for you to have fun during the curating process and have a joyous time when sharing the plants in a particular way with the people you appreciate.

Of course, if you have a friend who happens to be a stylist or an art curator, by all means, ask for their help. But if you don't, trust yourself and go with your gut and sense of style based on the purpose of your particular gathering.

When starting your curation process, which is selecting and organizing the plants you would like to show, exhibit, or present, think about why you feel compelled to do it. Is it because many of your friends have shown interest? Have you propagated a rare plant variety? Or, there is a magical flowering plant that you want others to experience with you? And if you're just using your plants as

Give your guests takeaways and information that's easy to remember, and stories they'll keep on telling others who weren't there.

an excuse to gather around them with a tight group of friends that's fine too.

Although I'm suggesting doing this for a personal display at home, this is a great project to do as part of a team-building experience at the workplace. Who knows—this could end up turning into a gardening club at the office.

Art experts suggest storytelling as a way to present your work during an exhibition (particularly if the artist is alive) to connect with your audience. In this case, think about which plants in your collection have compelling stories that you feel your guests will enjoy and engage with.

Besides the actual plants, you can add related objects that are linked directly to your plant collection or to your gardening lifestyle. These can be containers, tools, botanical prints, or others. You're in charge of this display!

Once you know what and how many objects you're presenting, think about the descriptions. As in a gallery where you can read or listen to the name of the artwork, details of the materials used, and facts that makes the art more interesting, you can do the same for your plant display. Here are some ideas that you can gather in writing or share orally with your guests about your plants and any other objects included in the display:

- The names of your plants, including their nicknames, common names, and botanical names
- Plant care tips
- A story (how did you acquire it, a gift, a loan with no return date, or a splurge?)

Once you decide on the final number of plants and objects to display, think about the location. It can be indoors or outdoors, or a mix of both, if you have the space. The location will also depend on what you're showing. Know this: your living room, your kitchen counter, or stairs make a great exhibition space.

Through time, I have gathered other objects, and probably you have, too, that can be useful for displaying your plants—from vintage birdcages and thick books to wooden blocks and cake stands. Let your creativity shine.

Use whatever is at your disposal: chairs, ladders, bookcases, clothing racks, the floor, and the ceilings. I'm fascinated every time I see plants hanging in front of a window (see "Hanging Planter Duo," page 38). When arranging your plants, play on top of surfaces, use a well-pressed tablecloth, in a solid color or a flashy one, that will complement a particular group of plants, or your whole collection.

Think about the lighting, too, in case you need to add some fixtures to enhance some beloved plants.

Remember that your personal collection, whether plants or other objects, is not just there exhibiting itself. It holds part of your essence; through it, you're sharing who you are, your style, what you care for, and the particular experiences that make each of the possessions special.

# Growing
# Gifts

Use your garden to harvest produce and
other natural supplies to create special
gifts to share with loved ones.

## PROJECT DESCRIPTION

I was beyond happy with the first pumpkin I ever harvested from my garden. I was in awe, excited, and grateful. And immediately, I was thinking about how I was going to share it. The pumpkin was big enough to divide into a few pieces. Half of it was to keep and prepare a couple of dishes for my family and the rest to gift away.

One of those pieces went to an advertising executive I was meeting with to sell her ad space for a coffee magazine I was producing back in the day. It wasn't a planned gift; I just felt generous, and confident to share something I was proud of. Needless to say, I sold the advertising for the magazine and our business relationship continued for a couple more years.

Sometimes, the gifts you have grown or made with your own hands can be more meaningful in the life of those who receive them. They open the door for new personal relationships or even propel business opportunities. You're not only giving a product, but you're also sharing part of who you are, your efforts and beliefs, and people will feel your appreciation.

Through the years, I have given many plants or produce from my gardening endeavors as gifts without a particular reason other than sharing, but I also have given planned green presents—from Mother's Day, Valentine's Day, and the holidays to my stepdaughters' life-changing moments, like leaving for college for the first time.

Your garden, including the one cultivated in containers, can become the best source of gifts you could ever ask for. I'm not telling you that all of your gifts have to be grown by you for now on, unless you want to, but at least a couple of them should be. You can reserve them for a special occasion or for special people.

Also, I like to collect fresh flowers and leaves from the trees and shrubs and press them for a

Nowadays, I use my garden to propagate plants that I can pot easily in beautiful containers, wait until they mature, then gift them forward.

few months to later use them to decorate postcards, bookmarks, or rock paperweights.

It's always fun to leave space for spontaneous gifts, but as you grow into your gardening lifestyle, planning some gifts ahead can also help keep you organized, imprint your personal brand, and stay on top of things stress-free, especially when it comes to gifts for particular occasions.

One of my latest interests is in harvesting and packaging seeds from my plants, as well as fresh herbs to dry and give as special mixes for tea

Cut branches of trees to use in fresh bouquets. The leaves of the silver mangrove (*Conocarpus erectus*) will contrast beautifully when combined with other colorful plants.

Dried branches of pennyroyal bush (*Mentha puligeum*) will make a fragrant and practical gift. They can be used as potpourri or hung over the shower for an aromatic bath experience.

If you already have a garden or want one, and you're looking for a theme or a new purpose for it, like growing your own gifts, I created this simple table to help you identify the type of gifts you want to grow and some potential ideas that can come from your future harvest.

I also included a blank table for you to personalize during your gift-generating process. Here, you can write about and plan your personal gifts, the occasion, the total amount of gifts needed, and other details that will help you determine your course of action, in and out of the garden, to have them ready by the time they're needed.

You don't need to create gifts for all the categories, just the ones you enjoy the most. I'm sure you will come up with new categories, too. And while your garden does its part, and you wait until harvest time, do an inventory in your home and look for packaging materials, like boxes, paper bags, ribbons, and any supplies that can be repurposed or useful to complete your gift presentation. Also include a list of supplies you will probably need to buy before your garden goods are ready to share. Place them in an easy-to-find drawer or closet.

And remember that the best gifts are those grown and made with love.

## Growing Your Own Gifts

### Fresh Goods
From plants great for making fresh-cut flower arrangements to just-harvested fruit, vegetables, herbs, seeds, or eggs from your happy chickens

### Propagated by You
From seedlings and transplants to well-thought-out plant containers

### Decorative Accents
From twigs, branches, and grasses to dried flowers, leaves, and fruits to use in decorating cards, wrappings, wreaths, or centerpieces

### Dry Goods
Edible herbs and flowers for tea recipes or potpourri mixes

### Added-Value Goods
The main ingredients for preparing the end gift, such as lemons to use in a custard or a cake recipe; fresh thyme or rosemary for baking cookies or bread, or making compound butters (also the eggs from your happy chickens); eggplants, tomatoes, or cucumbers for pickling

## Customizable Table of Gifts

Using the list on the previous page of the five types of grown gifts as a guide, create your own to-do list for a few *verduras*, knowing ahead of time what will you need from your garden or need to purchase.

| Type of Gift | Brief Description | How Many Are Needed | Date Needed | Preparation Time (hours/ days/months) |
|---|---|---|---|---|
| *Thanksgiving cards for work colleagues, etc.* | *pressing fig leaves to add to the cover of a card* | *15* | *November 13–17* | *1 month for pressing; 2 days for preparations; start early October* |
| | | | | |
| | | | | |
| | | | | |
| | | | | |
| | | | | |

# Additional Notes & Inspiration for Each Section

Pick your favorite project from each section and describe how you would adjust it for your own taste and circumstances. List materials and plants that you will use instead. Set a date to work on it.

## Explore Nature

---------------------------------

---------------------------------

---------------------------------

---------------------------------

---------------------------------

---------------------------------

---------------------------------

---------------------------------

---------------------------------

---------------------------------

---------------------------------

---------------------------------

---------------------------------

## Be Social

---------------------------------

---------------------------------

---------------------------------

---------------------------------

---------------------------------

---------------------------------

---------------------------------

---------------------------------

---------------------------------

---------------------------------

---------------------------------

---------------------------------

---------------------------------

# Encourage Wellness

---------------------------------

---------------------------------

---------------------------------

---------------------------------

---------------------------------

---------------------------------

---------------------------------

---------------------------------

---------------------------------

---------------------------------

---------------------------------

---------------------------------

---------------------------------

---------------------------------

---------------------------------

---------------------------------

---------------------------------

# Serve the Community

---------------------------------

---------------------------------

---------------------------------

---------------------------------

---------------------------------

---------------------------------

---------------------------------

---------------------------------

---------------------------------

---------------------------------

---------------------------------

---------------------------------

---------------------------------

---------------------------------

---------------------------------

---------------------------------

## Upcycle

-------------------------------------------

-------------------------------------------

-------------------------------------------

-------------------------------------------

-------------------------------------------

-------------------------------------------

-------------------------------------------

-------------------------------------------

-------------------------------------------

-------------------------------------------

-------------------------------------------

-------------------------------------------

-------------------------------------------

-------------------------------------------

-------------------------------------------

## Grow Into Your Own

-------------------------------------------

-------------------------------------------

-------------------------------------------

-------------------------------------------

-------------------------------------------

-------------------------------------------

-------------------------------------------

-------------------------------------------

-------------------------------------------

-------------------------------------------

-------------------------------------------

-------------------------------------------

-------------------------------------------

-------------------------------------------

-------------------------------------------

# Breaking Down the Gardening Process for Maximum Enjoyment

Add more joy to your life by knowing yourself and planning ahead for your gardening experiences.

## Project

Start by asking yourself what kind of gardening projects you want to experience (new or repeated) and think about the types you feel more drawn to or are curious to learn about. From hydroponics, bonsai, and orchids to container vegetable gardening or flowering ornamentals, there are many possibilities!

Ask yourself, or your friends, these questions:

- Why do I want to do this project? The answer could be that you want a specific gardening project accomplished, or about the gardening experience itself.
- Do you want a new hobby in your life?
- Are you looking for ways to reduce stress?
- Do you want to introduce your kids to gardening, and spend more time doing activities together?
- Do you need an activity to help you through a recovery process, or do you have a vocational purpose?

Finally, assess your physical strength and capabilities to tackle the project, or whether you will need assistance from start to finish.

These are important questions whose answers will help you have a clearer view of the project's outcome.

Always put yourself in a winning position and adjust the project to your needs. The more joy and satisfaction you experience, the more excited you will be to continue gardening.

## Timing

To increase the potential of having a great time gardening, and wanting to continue the activity, select when and how it is best suited for you.

- Is gardening something you want to do daily, a couple of days a week, or just on weekends?
- Do you prefer early mornings before anyone else is up? Or after work as a transitional activity to home chores, or late at night after everybody is asleep?
- How much time do you want to devote to gardening? Minutes or hours?

Knowing these important details will make it easier for you to find the right garden project and schedule time for it. Depending on the project, it may need to be split into two or more parts to be completed. Be flexible about the process to reduce disappointment and to maintain the feeling that you have it under control.

Your *why* for your garden project will help you determine how much time to invest in it.

## Resources

Your gardening preferences, and frequency, will determine the amount and kind of resources you will need to continue with your experiences. When conceptualizing any project, first do some research about the basic materials needed and their costs.

Before buying anything, do an inventory at home or consider strategies such as purchasing secondhand products (containers, tools, accessories), bartering, or partnering with a garden buddy to lower the costs of gardening goods.

If gardening is going to be your go-to hobby, consider creating a monthly budget to cover essential materials, plants, books, workshops, garden club memberships, and other opportunities that will arise without compromising other household responsibilities.

## Space

Think about the space you're currently in and the kinds of projects you would like to do as well as your mobility and strength to accomplish them. These factors will also determine the type of furniture, paths, and accessories needed to facilitate a safe and comfortable experience.

If you're planning to spend a considerable amount of time gardening, indoors or outdoors, it's helpful to have a permanent, safe, and accessible area to do so, such as a garden shed or gardening station with your gardening equipment at hand.

Always consider proper and safe storage for your gardening tools, accessories, fertilizers, soil bags, and semi-completed projects as well. When space is a challenge and you're using the dinner table, countertops, or other multipurpose surfaces for your gardening projects, keep your materials even more organized to help you clean up fast and minimize disruption to the other activities that go on in those spaces (see "Indoor Garden Shed," page 116, for ideas to organize your gardening materials).

If a particular gardening project has no room at your house, don't be discouraged. Look for alternative spaces to fulfill your *verduras* craving, such as a community garden, a friend's home, or your workplace.

### Gardening, Step by Step

Every gardening project starts with one single action. Use this list to start gardening as soon as possible. By completing one action at a time, you'll feel the progress of each gardening endeavor you set out to complete.

#### GATHERING

1. Inspiration/sketching
2. Materials/accessories
3. Tools needed

#### ORGANIZING

1. Decide where to do the activity.
2. Acquire any furniture needed.
3. Coordinate any assistance (if applicable).
4. Schedule the project in your calendar.

#### ASSEMBLING

1. Gather all needed materials in your work area.
2. Garden and enjoy the process.
3. Clean up and store any tools and supplies left over.
4. Place the finished project in a safe area with easy access to keep up with its maintenance.

# Gardening Project Plants and Plant Alternatives

## Explore Nature

| GARDEN PROJECT | PLANT NAME (Common & Botanical Names) | USE FOR | PLANT ALTERNATIVES |
| --- | --- | --- | --- |
| **Gardening with Your Thirteen-Year-Old Self** | Caladium, *Caladium* | Thriller | Stingray, *Alocasia macrorrhiza* 'Stingray' |
| | Wax begonia, *Begonia semperflorens* | Filler | Silver ripple peperomia, *Peperomia caperata* |
| | Gray artillery plant, *Pilea glaucophylla* | Ground cover | Gold spikemoss, *Selaginella kraussiana* |
| **Wonder Bowl Garden** | Angel's tears, *Soleirolia soleiroii* | Ground cover, carpet | Corsican mint, *Mentha requienii* |
| **Night Sky Garden** | Gold lace cactus, *Mammillaria elongate* | Grouped plants | Venus flytrap, *Dionaea muscipula* |
| | Snowball cactus, *Mammillaria candida* | Rounded feature/ concept | Moon cactus, *Gymnocalycium mihanovichii* |
| | *Gasteraloe* | Starred or rosette feature | Hens and chicks, *Sempervivum tectorum* |
| | *Juniperus procumbens* | Creeping feature | Creeping Siberian cypress, *Microbiota decussata* |
| **Miniature Garden** | Common asparagus fern, *Asparagus plumosus* | Tree | Parlor palm, *Chamaedorea elegans* |
| | Common ivy, *Hedera helix* | Vine | Maidenhair vine, *Muehlenbeckia axillaris* |
| | Foxtail fern, *Asparagus densiflorus;* Sedum | Shrub | Jade plant, *Crassula* spp. |
| | Gray artillery plant, *Pilea glaucophylla* | Ground cover | Creeping sedum, *Sedum* spp. |

## Be Social

| GARDEN PROJECT | PLANT NAME (Common & Botanical Names) | USE FOR | PLANT ALTERNATIVES |
|---|---|---|---|
| **Hanging Planter Duo** | *Rhaphidophora tetrasperma* | Spiller, filler | Philodendron, *Philodendron cordatum* |
| | Swiss cheese plant, *Monstera adansonii* | Spiller, filler | N'joy pothos, *Epipremnum aureum 'n'joy'* |
| **Little Library Garden** | Golden trumpet, *Allamanda cathartica* | Filler, flowers | Carolina lupine, *Thermopsis villosa* |
| | Portulaca, *Portulaca* | Ground cover, spiller, flowers | Sea thrift, *Armeria maritima* |

## Encourage Wellness

| GARDEN PROJECT | PLANT NAME (Common & Botanical Names) | USE FOR | PLANT ALTERNATIVES |
|---|---|---|---|
| **Barefoot Garden** | Lemon thyme, *Thymus citriodorus* | Ground cover | Dwarf chamomile, *Chamaemelum nobile* 'Treneague' or Roman chamomile, *Chamaemelum nobile* |
| **Sofrito Garden** | Culantro, *Eryngium foetidum* | Filler, herb, edible | Cilantro (coriander), *Coriandrum sativum* |
| | *Capsicum chinense* | Thriller, fruit, edible | Tomato, *Lycopersicum esculentum* |
| **Meditation Garden** | Copperleaf, *Acalypha wilkesiana* | Shrub/privacy | Cranberry hibiscus or false Jamaican rose hibiscus, *Hibiscus acetosella* |
| | Fountain grass, *Pennisetum setaceum* | Shrub/privacy, movement | Ornamental bamboo, *Pleioblastus shibuyanus* 'Tsuboi' |

## Serve the Community

| GARDEN PROJECT | PLANT NAME (Common & Botanical Names) | USE FOR | PLANT ALTERNATIVES |
|---|---|---|---|
| **Garden Lift** | Lemon ball sedum, *Sedum rupestre* | Filler, spiller | Angelina stonecrop, *Sedum rupestre* 'Angelina' |
| | Fountain grass, *Pennisetum* spp. | Filler | Blue fescue, *Festuca glauca* |
| | Mandevilla, *Mandevilla* | Flowering vine | Clematis, *Clematis* |
| | Papyrus, *Cyperus papyrus* | Thriller | Umbrella palm, *Cyperus alternifolius* |
| | Dense-flowered loosestrife, *Lysimachia congestiflora* | Filler, spiller | Creeping thyme, *Thymus praecox* |
| **Healing Nook** | Red Panama rose, *Rondeletia strigose* | Flowering shrub | Butterfly bush, *Buddleia davidii* |
| | Lemon ball sedum, *Sedum rupestre* | Ground cover | Murale sedum, *Sedum album* 'Murale' |
| | Fountain grass, *Pennisetum* spp. | Filler, flowing plant | Mexican feather grass, *Stipa tenuissima* |
| | Firecracker plant, *Cuphea* | Pollinator plant | Pure Joy sedum, *Hylotelephium* 'Pure Joy' |
| | Coleus, *Coleus* | Foliage plant | Croton, *Codiaeum variegatum* |

## Upcycle

| GARDEN PROJECT | PLANT NAME (Common & Botanical Names) | USE FOR | PLANT ALTERNATIVES |
|---|---|---|---|
| Candelabra Plant Holder | *Sedum adolphii* | Spike, concept | Fire stick cactus, *Euphorbia tirucalli* |
| Swinging Planter | Wax begonia, *Begonia semperflorens* | Filler | Coral bells, *Heuchera* |
| | Beetle peperomia, *Peperomia quadrangularis* | Spiller | Creeping fig, *Ficus pumila* |
| | Heart fern, *Hemionitis arifolia* | Thriller | Maidenhair fern, *Adiantum raddianum* |

## Grow into Your Own

| GARDEN PROJECT | PLANT NAME (Common & Botanical Names) | USE FOR | PLANT ALTERNATIVES |
|---|---|---|---|
| Create a Living Background for Virtual Meetings | 'Silver Satin' pothos, *Scindapsus pictus* | Vine | Heartleaf philodendron, *Philodendron hederaceum* 'Brasil' |
| Garden Art Installation in a Bonsai Dish | Wax begonia, *Begonia semperflorens* | Filler | Hosta, *Hosta sieboldiana* 'Frances Williams' |
| | Angel's tears, *Soleirolia soleiroii* | Ground cover | Baby tears, *Pilea depressa* |
| | Silver ripple peperomia, *Peperomia caperata* | Filler, spiller | Watermelon peperomia, *Peperomia argyreia* |

# References

Griffiths, A., and M. Keightley. *Your Well-Being Garden: How to Make Your Garden Good for You—Science, Design, Practice.* London: DK, 2020.

Haller, R. L., and C. L. Capra, eds. *Horticultural Therapy Methods: Connecting People and Plants in Health Care, Human Services, and Therapeutic Programs.* 2nd ed. Boca Raton, FL: CRC Press, 2017.

Haller, R. L., K. L. Kennedy, and C. L. Capra. *The Profession and Practice of Horticultural Therapy.* Boca Raton, FL: CRC Press, 2019.

Simson, S., and M. Straus. *Horticulture as Therapy: Principles and Practice.* Boca Raton, FL: CRC Press, 2003.

## Explore Nature

### WONDER BOWL GARDEN

Louv, Richard. *Last Child in the Woods: Saving Our Children from Nature-Deficit Disorder.* Updated and expanded ed. Chapel Hill, NC and New York City: Algonquin Books, 2022.

United States Environmental Protection Agency. "Indoor Air Quality." September 7, 2021. www.epa.gov/report-environment/indoor-air-quality.

### COASTAL GARDEN

BlueHealth. "Getting Office-Workers Walking." (n.d.) https://bluehealth2020.eu/projects/walking-workers/.

Clark, J. "Trees for the Beach." *Tips Bulletin.* May 13, 2021. www.tipsbulletin.com/trees-for-the-beach/.

NASA Science. "Living Ocean." (n.d.) https://science.nasa.gov/earth-science/oceanography/living-ocean.

National Oceanic and Atmospheric Administration, Office for Coastal Management. "Puerto Rico." (n.d.) https://coast.noaa.gov/states/puerto-rico.html.

Pearson, A., R. Bottomley, T. Chambers, L. Thornton, J. Stanley, M. Smith, et al. "Measuring Blue Space Visibility and 'Blue Recreation' in the Everyday Lives of Children in a Capital City." *International Journal of Environmental Research and Public Health* 14, no. 6 (2017): 563. https://doi.org/10.3390/ijerph14060563.

Thompson & Morgan. "Plants for Coastal and Exposed Gardens." ( n.d.) www.thompson-morgan.com/plants-for-coastal-gardens.

### NIGHT SKY GARDEN

Fuller, Taylor. "Bioluminescent Plants Are the Next Big Thing." *The Spruce.* September 20, 2022. www.thespruce.com/bioluminescent-plants-next-big-thing-6274445.

Harden, O. "New Study Officially Found the Place with the Least Light Pollution in the World." *Matador Network.* August 17, 2022. https://matadornetwork.com/read/new-study-officially-found-place-least-light-pollution-world/.

International Dark-Sky Association. "Light Pollution." February 14, 2017. www.darksky.org/light-pollution/.

International Dark-Sky Association. "Night Sky Heritage." May 7, 2019. www.darksky.org/light-pollution/night-sky-heritage/.

The Arecibo Observatory. Landing Page. (n.d.) www.naic.edu/ao/landing.

### MINIATURE GARDEN

Elzer-Peters, K. *Miniature Gardens: Design and Create Miniature Fairy Gardens, Dish Gardens, Terrariums, and More—Indoors and Out.* Beverly, MA: Cool Springs Press, 2014.

Manda, M. "Miniature Landscapes." *Annals of the University of Craiova* 20, no. 56 (2015). www.researchgate.net/profile/Manuela-Manda/publication/292762750_MINIATURE_LANDSCAPES/links/56b102ea08ae56d7b069cc70/MINIATURE-LANDSCAPES.pdf.

Penn Medicine News. "Yoga, Running, Weight Lifting, and Gardening: Penn Study Maps the Types of Physical Activity Associated with Better Sleep Habits." June 4, 2015. www.pennmedicine.org/news/news-releases/2015/june/yoga-running-weight-lifting-an.

## Be Social

Chalmin-Pui, Lauriane Suyin, Alistair Griffiths, Jenny Roe, Timothy Heaton, and Ross Cameron. "Why Garden?—Attitudes and the Perceived Health Benefits of Home Gardening." *Cities* 112, no. 103118. (2021). https://doi.org/10.1016/j.cities.2021.103118.

Schattenberg, Paul. "The Positive Effects of Gardening on Mental Health." *Texas A&M Today*. May 16, 2022. https://today.tamu.edu/2022/05/18/the-positive-effects-of-gardening-on-mental-health/.

Thompson, R. "Gardening for Health: A Regular Dose of Gardening." *Clinical Medicine* 18, no. 3 (June 2018): 201–205. https://doi.org/10.7861/clinmedicine.18-3-201.

### A GARDEN GATHERING AT HOME

Parker, P. *The Art of Gathering: How We Meet and Why It Matters*. (reprint ed.) New York City: Riverhead Books, 2020.

### LITTLE LIBRARY GARDEN

Little Free Library. "How to Site and Install a Little Free Library Book Exchange." September 13, 2017. www.youtube.com/watch?v=eKgQ8o6BUUw

Little Free Library. "Take a Book. Share a Book." November 16, 2022. https://littlefreelibrary.org/.

Neuman, S. B., and J. J. Knapczyk. "Reaching Families Where They Are: Examining an Innovative Book Distribution Program." *Urban Education* 55, no. 4 (2020): 542–569. https://doi.org/10.1177/0042085918770722.

Salem, T. "Proximity to Books Enhances Children's Learning." *US News*. May 3, 2018. www.usnews.com/news/national-news/articles/2018-05-03/proximity-to-books-enhances-childrens-learning.

Stevenson, R. "Make Your Library ADA Friendly, Not Just ADA Compliant." *Public Libraries Online*. (n.d.) https://publiclibrariesonline.org/2021/06/make-your-library-ada-friendly-not-just-ada-compliant/.

United States Department of Education. "Access to Reading Materials." (n.d.) www2.ed.gov/datastory/bookaccess/index.html.

### BRING YOUR HERB COCKTAIL AND MOCKTAIL GARDEN BAR ANYWHERE

Gold, Betty. "How to Incorporate Fresh Garden Herbs into Cocktails." *Real Simple.* May 20, 2020. www.realsimple.com/food-recipes/cooking-tips-techniques/preparation/cocktails-with-herbs.

Peña López, J. "Coctelería para tus fiestas navideñas." *Agrochic: Jardinería Y Bienestar*. November 16, 2021. https://agrochic.com/cocteleria-para-tus-fiestas-navidenas/.

### SAY IT WITH *VERDURA*!

Kumar, A., and N. Epley. "Undervaluing Gratitude: Expressers Misunderstand the Consequences of Showing Appreciation." *Psychological Science* 29, no. 9 (2018): 1423–1435. https://doi.org/10.1177/0956797618772506.

Murphy, H. "You Should Actually Send That Thank You Note You've Been Meaning to Write." *The New York Times*. January 24, 2020. www.nytimes.com/2018/07/20/science/thank-you-notes.html.

O'Flaherty, Shibeal, Michael T. Sanders, and Ashley Whillans. "Research: A Little Recognition Can Provide a Big Morale Boost." *Harvard Business Review*. September 17, 2021. https://hbr.org/2021/03/research-a-little-recognition-can-provide-a-big-morale-boost?autocomplete=true.

# Encourage Wellness

Das, L. T. "What Science Tells Us about the Mood-Boosting Effects of Indoor Plants." *Washington Post*. June 7, 2022. www.washingtonpost.com/wellness/2022/06/06/how-houseplants-can-boost-your-mood/.

Fleming, Lesley, Amy Davis, Lana Bos, Janet Carter, and Beth House. "Nova Scotia's Horticulture for Health Activities." *Journal of Therapeutic Horticulture* 30, no. 1 (2020):56–65.

### ROOM WITH A VIEW

Bugos, C. "This Website Highlights Views Outside Windows Across the World." *Smithsonian Magazine*. July 16, 2020. www.smithsonianmag.com/smart-news/window-swap-180975334/.

Government of Western Australia, Department of Health. "Intensive Care Units (ICUs)." HealthyWA. (n.d.) www.healthywa.wa.gov.au/Articles/F_I/Intensive-care-units-ICUs.

Ulrich, R. S. "View Through a Window May Influence Recovery from Surgery." *Science* 224, no. 4647 (1984): 420–421. https://doi.org/10.1126/science.6143402.

WindowSwap. "The Calmest Place on the Internet." (n.d.) www.window-swap.com/.

### BAREFOOT GARDEN

Bindu, B., and G. santoshkumar. "Physiological Changes with Middle Aged Women Due to Brisk Walking on Grass." *International Journal of Physical Education, Sports and Health* 5, no. 2 (2018): 70–72.

Colborn, N. *Garden Floor: From Gravel Gardens to Chamomile Lawns.* Trafalgar Square Pub., 2022.

Gardener's Supply Company. "Thyme." (n.d.) www.gardeners.com/how-to/thyme/7208.html.

Harvard Health. "Foot Massage: The Pause That Refreshes and Is Good for You!" December 26, 2014. www.health.harvard.edu/mind-and-mood/foot-massage-the-pause-that-refreshes-and-it-good-for-you.

Lindberg, S. "Does Walking Barefoot Have Health Benefits?" *Healthline.* March 8, 2019, www.healthline.com/health/walking-barefoot.

Wilde, K. "The Amazing Ripple Effect of Foot Rolling." *Wild Peace.* December 1, 2018. www.wildpeace.org/the-boost/2018/11/30/the-amazing-ripple-effect-of-foot-rolling.

### SOFRITO GARDEN

Cuadra, C. M. O. *Puerto Rico en la olla: somos aún lo que comimos?* Aranjuez (Madrid), Spain: Ediciones Doce Calles, 2006.

Pálsdóttir, A. M., L. O'Brien, D. Varning Poulsen, and A. Dolling. "Exploring a Migrant's Sense of Belonging Through Participation in an Urban Agricultural Vocational Training Program in Sweden." *Journal of Therapeutic Horticulture* 31, no. 1 (January 2021): 10–23.

### MEDITATION GARDEN

Behan, C. "The Benefits of Meditation and Mindfulness Practices During Times of Crisis such as COVID-19." *Irish Journal of Psychological Medicine* 37, no. 4 (2020): 256–258. https://doi.org/10.1017/ipm.2020.38.

Han, B. C. *Loa a la Tierra.* Barcelona: Herder, 2021.

Locher, M., and K. Bartholomew. "On the Restorative Power of Nature, or Why Every Neighborhood Needs a Public Japanese Garden." *Journal of Comparative Urban Law and Policy* 5, no 1 (2022): 528–538.

Lynn, B. "How to Design a Meditation Garden." *Horticulture.* April 13, 2020. www.hortmag.com/gardens/meditation-garden.

Mayo Clinic. "Meditation: A Simple, Fast Way to Reduce Stress." April 29, 2022. www.mayoclinic.org/tests-procedures/meditation/in-depth/meditation/art-20045858.

M. L. Harvey, K. Bowman, and A. Karr. "The Gardening Spirit: Evidence That Frequency of Gardening Precisely Predicts Ecospirituality." *Journal of Therapeutic Horticulture* 31, no. 1 (2021).

## Serve the Community

### GARDEN LIFT

Browning, Bill, Chris Garvin, Catie Ryan, Namita Kallianpurkar, Leslie Labruto, Siobhan Watson, et al. "The Economics of Biophilia." (2012). Terrapin Bright Green. Accessed December 14, 2022. www.terrapinbrightgreen.com/report/economics-of-biophilia/.

### GARDEN BREAK ROOM

Moss, J. "Beyond Burned Out." *Harvard Business Review.* November 8, 2022. https://hbr.org/2021/02/beyond-burned-out.

## Upcycle

Caprioli, Sara, Christoph Fuchs, and Bram Van den Bergh. "The Appeal of Upcycled Products: The Role of Perceived Creativity," in *NA—Advances in Consumer Research* 47 (2019): 487–488. eds. Bagchi Rajesh, Lauren Block, and Leonard Lee. Duluth, MN: Association for Consumer Research.

Dickie, G. "Landfills Around the World Release a Lot of Methane—Study." Reuters. August 11, 2022. www.reuters.com/business/environment/landfills-around-world-release-lot-methane-study-2022-08-10/.

Grant, B. L. "Garden Upcycling Ideas: Learn about Upcycling in the Garden." *Gardening Know How.* February 6, 2022. www.gardeningknowhow.com/garden-how-to/projects/garden-upcycling-ideas.htm.

### SWINGING PLANTER

Moore, B. H. "The True Stories Behind Beauty and The Beast and Other Disney Stories." *BBC News.* March 18, 2017. www.bbc.com/news/newsbeat-39302636.

## Grow into Your Own

Eng, S., T., Khun, S., Jower, and M. J. Murro. "Healthy Lifestyle Through Home Gardening: The Art of Sharing." *American Journal of Lifestyle Medicine* 13, no. 4 (2019): 347–350. https://doi.org/10.1177/1559827619842068.

## CREATE A LIVING BACKGROUND FOR VIRTUAL MEETINGS

Boutin, Chad. "Snap Judgments Decide a Face's Character, Psychologist Finds." Princeton University. August 22, 2006. www.princeton.edu/news/2006/08/22/snap-judgments-decide-faces-character-psychologist-finds?section=topstories.

Gallo, Carmine. "How to Create a Professional Setup for Virtual Meetings." *Inc.com*. (n.d.) www.inc.com/carmine-gallo/how-to-create-a-professional-setup-for-virtual-meetings.html.

Kuseybi, R. "Interior Design Tips for Your Zoom Meeting." Vishion. August 21, 2020. https://vishion.co/interior-design-tips-for-your-zoom-meeting/.

Marbella International University Centre. "The Importance of a Proper Zoom/Google Hangout Background." Marbella International University Centre. June 10, 2021. https://miuc.org/background-in-virtual-meetings/.

Mautz, Scott. "Want to Make a Great First Impression? A Princeton Psychologist Says Be Aware of 3 Snap Judgments People Make." *Inc.com*. (n.d.) www.inc.com/scott-mautz/a-princeton-psychologist-says-people-make-these-3-snap-judgments-within-milliseconds-of-meeting-you.html.

Steele, Lauren. "Got an Important Zoom Meeting? We've Got Six Tips for Dressing Up Your Background, from an Interior Designer." *Fast Company*. July 27, 2020. www.fastcompany.com/90528067/got-an-important-zoom-coming-up-here-are-six-tips-to-dress-up-your-background-from-an-interior-designer.

The College of Optometrists. "Screen Use." (n.d.) https://lookafteryoureyes.org/eye-care/screen-use/.

Zoom. "Your Year on Zoom." October 7, 2022. https://explore.zoom.us/en/zoom-user-survey/.

## LEGACY GARDEN

Stuart-Smith, S. *The Well-Gardened Mind: The Restorative Power of Nature*. New York City: Scribner, 2021.

## GARDEN ART INSTALLATION IN A BONSAI DISH

Hölldobler Bert, and E. O. Wilson. *Journey to the Ants: A Story of Scientific Exploration*. Cambridge, MA: Belknap Press of Harvard University Press, 1994.

Odeh, R., E. R. M. Diehl, S. J. Nixon, C. C. Tisher, D. Klempner, J. K. Sonke, et al. "A Pilot Randomized Controlled Trial of Group-Based Indoor Gardening and Art Activities Demonstrates Therapeutic Benefits to Healthy Women." *PLOS ONE* 17, no. 7 (2022): e0269248. https://doi.org/10.1371/journal.pone.0269248.

Puiu, T. "How Gardening Reduces Depression Symptoms and Improves Mental Health." ZME Science. October 20, 2022. www.zmescience.com/science/news-science/how-gardening-reduces-depression-symptoms-and-improves-mental-health/.

## DISPLAY YOUR FAVORITE PLANTS

Homes & Antiques. "10 Ways to Display Art in Your Home." November 11, 2022. www.homesandantiques.com/ antiques/display-ideas/10-ways-to-display-art-in-your-home/.

Richardson, J. "How Can Museums Use Their Collection to Connect to Audiences?" *MuseumNext* . August 11, 2022. www.museumnext.com/article/7-ways-to-use-your-collection-to-connect-to-audiences/.

# Note of Appreciation

WHAT AN INCREDIBLE, humbling, and memorable experience putting together this book was. Thank you to my editor, Jessica Walliser, for her vision and kindest guidance, and to the amazing team at Quarto who made this beautiful book possible, in English and in Spanish at once.

Thank you to photographer, Jorge Ramírez Portela, who I had worked with previously, but never at this level of intensity. I'm grateful he said yes. Not only is he talented, a nature lover, and a well-known photographer, but Jorge is also a professional, funny, and reliable person. His beautiful photos helped me see my garden in a different light, literally, and to love even more what I do every day.

A particular thank you to my dear friends: Abra Lee, for her constant support and words of advice, way before this book journey started; Julie Power, for reading the first sample pages of this book and giving me her favorable opinions; and Vivian Sánchez, for saying yes to opening her home for the first book's photoshoot, even though COVID made us cancel it, her enthusiasm and friendship over so many years have been meaningful to my life.

Also, I want to thank my friend and media colleague Carly Carrión for taking the time to build the little library bookcase (see page 46). It's incredible how many things you can learn and make from two wood panels, an acrylic sheet, and some hi-tech tools, of course, if you have the guidance and patience of someone like him who knows what to do.

I can't thank my family enough. To my parents, whose support is everything. Thank you for your understanding and for instilling in me the love for books, nature, and the importance of local agriculture for our well-being.

And very importantly, to my husband, Antonio. To have a partner that understands your passion is everything. This has been his journey, too. Thank you for bringing lunch to the photoshoots; for listening, patiently, to my many ideas, and to some of my frustrations when things were not going my way. Your opinion always matters to me.

Thanks to my stepdaughters, Sofía and Verónica, for taking me into your already-started lives and letting me show you one or two things about life and gardening. I'm a very proud stepmother.

And lastly, to my readers, followers, and business partners. Thank you for your immense support over the years to *Agrochic* and my other gardening-related projects that have brought me to these pages. Thank you for doing the same for this book. Wishing you many great *verduras* and a blissful time with the people you care about and love.

# Meet Perla Sofía

**Perla Sofía Curbelo-Santiago** was born and raised in Puerto Rico, where she lives currently. She is a gardener and a passionate advocate for using gardening for well-being. A professional communicator and founder of *Agrochic.com*, a gardening lifestyle platform in Spanish, Perla Sofía possesses both a sweet tooth and a bachelor's degree in psychology from the University of Puerto Rico (UPRM), a master's degree in public relations from Universidad del Sagrado Corazón, and a Horticultural Therapy Certificate from the Chicago Botanic Garden.

In 2021, she was recognized by the American Horticultural Society (AHS) with the B. Y. Morrison Communication Award. As a media contributor, her work has appeared in several publications from Puerto Rico and the United States, such as *El Nuevo Día*, *HipLatina*, *Garden Center Magazine*, and *The American Gardener*. She is also a gardening television contributor.

Perla Sofia is affiliated with several organizations, including Garden Communicators International, the American Horticultural Therapy Association (AHTA), American Horticultural Society (AHS), BIPOC Hort Group, and *Asociación Española de Horticultura y Jardinería Social y Terapéutica* (AEHJST). In 2022, she joined the Board of Directors of KidsGardening.org.

Besides Spanish and English, she speaks fluent Italian and wants to keep learning other languages. As a kid, she dreamed of working for the United Nations as a translator. Connect with Perla Sofía at Agrochic.com and on social media: Facebook (@Agrochic), Twitter (@perlasofia), and Instagram (@agrochic).

# Index

Page numbers in **bold** indicate illustrations